TAI CHI AND THE
ART OF MINDFULNESS

ALSO BY MITCH GOLDFARB

DO LESS – ACHIEVE MORE
A Guided Audio Textbook of
"Professor Cheng Man-Ching's
Simplified 37-Posture Tai Chi Form"

NATIVE PATH
Goldfarb has written and produced numerous healing and meditation CDs,
including five for Dr. Deepak Chopra. *Native Path*, music for Tai Chi, yoga and
meditation is available on iTunes.

EMBRACING ABUNDANCE
Mitch Goldfarb's writing and production helped to create the Living
Consciously By Design meditation and mindful living series, *Embracing
Abundance*. In this five CD collection, Goldfarb teams with spiritual leader
Normand René Poulin to create a guided meditation experience like no other.

ARTICLES ON TAI CHI AND MEDITATION
Professor Goldfarb's articles can be found in several publications.

Tai Chi and the
Art of Mindfulness

A Ch'i Essential Workbook

Mitch Goldfarb

COPYRIGHT

Author's website: http://www.mitchgoldfarb.com/taichiarts

Published in the United States 2015 by
Sound Soul Publishing, Downingtown, PA 19335
Printed by Create Space

ISBN-13: 978-1514288740

ISBN-10: 1514288745

1.Mindfulness 2.Tai Chi 3.Mind-Body-Spirit 4.Inspiration 5.Psychology 6.Spirituality 7.Self-Help 8.Personal Growth 9.Meditation 10.Lifestyle & Wellness 11.Health

FIRST EDITION, 2015

"No matter what accomplishments you make, somebody helps you."

WILMA RUDOLPH

Art of Mindfulness Special Thanks and Gratitude List

CREATIVITY DOES NOT HAPPEN IN A VACUUM. It comes about through inter-actions with ideas, philosophies, and most of all people. It is to these people—the ones who interacted with the material in this workbook, its presentation, its accessibility, as well as, of course, with me—that I remain humbled and entirely grateful. It is their contributions that helped create *Tai Chi and the Art of Mindfulness*.

These contributors helped share my vision of the mindfulness Tai Chi brings to the world. They stoked my excitement to push the envelope. I wish to thank them all for their dedication and outstanding work.

First, there is my beautiful bride, Jeanne, my best friend, Spirit lifter, and co-conspirator in sharing this wonderful journey. Thank you for being a first reader, and for safeguarding my space to work and focus, even when I was deep down the rabbit hole. You are always there and always a bright light.

Meyer D. Goldfarb, my father, thanks for being a first reader and having an amazing command of the English language at 97-years-young. Thanks for your inspiration and the work ethic both you and Mom have instilled in me. It has gotten me over the humps and speed bumps along the road.

Grandmaster Maggie Newman for opening my eyes and heart to the loving feelings that our Tai Chi has to offer the world. Her tales, wisdom, and inspiration have lit the way for so many of us. With grace and elegance, she shares the magic of Tai Chi.

Jano Cohen, friend, Master Tai Chi instructor, and senior student of Grandmaster Maggie Newman, has contributed more than she knows to my deeper understanding of using *ch'i*, Sword Form, and is owed another debt of thanks for introducing me to Ms. Newman. Jano always knows the right inspiring thing to say to help me continue raising the bar of my Tai Chi practice. Visit her website: www.alexandertechnique-teacher.com

"You have no cause for anything but gratitude and joy."

THE BUDDHA

David-Dorian Ross, friend and International Master Tai Chi instructor, for his wonderful teachings, inspiration, humor, and play, as well as taking Tai Chi to a new level of enjoyment. Mr. Ross's ideas and approach to living the Tai Chi principles in daily life has helped push the envelope of my joy of the exploration of Tai Chi. Visit his website: www.daviddorianross.com

Alison Donley, friend, colleague at West Chester University, and Master yoga instructor, for sharing her knowledge and wisdom in creating a workbook. Ms. Donley is an inspiration in mindfulness as evident by her students and anyone who has met her. Visit her website: www.thelightwithinyoga.com

Paul Bronaugh, designer and graduate of West Chester University, for his design expertise and patience in sharing the ins and outs of the software used to lay out this workbook. Mr. Bronaugh's thumbprint is part of the beauty each page holds.

Dr. Bessie Lawton, friend and colleague at West Chester University, and her mother, Grace Hsieh-Hsing, for proofing the Chinese characters, the hanzi, used in this workbook.

Dr. Eleanor F. Shevlin, friend and colleague at West Chester University, for her direction and oversight in editing this workbook. Her generosity, knowledge, and dedication, both to her students and this project, lifted the bar to create the book you read today. Please visit the website below for information about not only the Center for Book History but also the Graduate Certificate in Publishing and its related editing services and prepublication assistance. www.wcupa.edu/BookHistory

Dr. Jen Bacon, friend and colleague at West Chester University, for putting me in touch with Dr. Eleanor F. Shevlin. Over the years, Dr. Bacon has been a constant source of insight and direction.

Mary Freed, editor and graduate assistant to Dr. Shevlin, for her hands-on contribution with each and every page. Mary's attention to detail as well as her thoughtful suggestions improved the presentation of the material herein. I remain very grateful for her input.

Jean Piper Burton, Associate Professor of Library Services at West Chester University, for her help and direction in cataloging for the Library of Congress.

I wish to offer an extra special note of thanks and gratitude to Dr. Ray Zetts for his vision in introducing Tai Chi as part of the curriculum at West Chester University. And to Dr. Frank Fry, as well as the Dean of the College of Health Sciences, Dr. Linda Adams, for supporting the progressive programs the University has to offer our students in Contemplative Studies.

Dr. Don McCown, friend and colleague at West Chester University, for his encouragement and support. Dr. Don McCown is the Director of the Center for Contemplative Studies and the Program Director for the Contemplative Studies minor.

Jeff Hennelly, friend and writing cohort, for being a trusted first reader.

J. Paul Simeone, friend, photographer, videographer, musician and artist extraordinaire, for assistance with and guidance on the cover image. Mr. Simeone is also the photographer of the author photo on the back cover. Visit his website: www.jpaulsimeone.com

Jonathan Maberry, *New York Times* bestselling author and winner of multiple Bram Stoker Awards, for his generosity and teachings in the art of writing. Visit his website: www.jonathanmaberry.com

Dr. Bernie Siegel, bestselling author of *The Art of Healing* and *365 Prescriptions For The Soul*, for his generosity of Spirit, inspiration, as well as the kindness and light he brought to my mother and family in a difficult time. Visit his website for wonderful articles, books, and CDs. www.berniesiegelmd.com

"If the only prayer you said was thank you, that would be enough."

MEISTER ECKHART

Ten thousand flowers in Spring, the moon in Autumn,
A cool breeze in Summer, snow in Winter.
If your mind isn't clouded by unnecessary things,
This is the best season of your life.

WU-MEN
ANCIENT CHINESE SAGE

THIS BOOK IS DEDICATED TO . . .

To Jeanne, for her love, insight, and always raising the bar of empowerment. Her joy of embracing life is as contagious as it is energizing.

To all my students. You inspire me to dig deeper, grow more, and are the reason for this book. Thank you.

實現

LIVE THE DREAM

CONTENTS

Foreword

BERNARD S. SIEGEL, MD

TAI CHI AND THE ART OF MINDFULNESS is an incredible source of wisdom and one of the greatest life coaches I have ever seen. Of course, you must understand I am saying this because I agree with every word and lesson this book contains. Very honestly, I would recommend that it replace the Ten Commandments because of its practical nature, wisdom and ease of application.

To truly comment about how I felt after reading through it would require my writing a book about how meaningful all these topics and lessons have been in my life. It speaks the TRUTH, something many of us want to deny but which we all need to face and learn to accept. When we know our life's story, then we know the truth because only a story is truer than the truth. When we live and love, we create what I call "LIOVE." I coined this word to share the unity of living and loving. When we touch others, they understand our message and are aware of the life-changing capacity of "MEASSAGE," another of my created words.

Dreaming, truth, living, loving, and letting our heart make up our mind all will lead us to our true path and to our life's journey. One of the most significant points mentioned in the book is about stillness, something most of us do not appreciate as we seek distractions to avoid the truth. Over and over myths and fairy tales speak to us of the STILL POND. Why? Because when the waters of our minds are turbulent, our minds are using us and controlling our lives, but when we create the still pond,

it allows us to see our true reflection without the distortion and lack of clarity created by the turbulence of life's distractions. The still pond enables the ugly duckling to see he is a swan, and a tiger raised by goats to see his truth, that he is a tiger. So read on and quiet your mind and find your true self. Let your consciousness speak to you through dreams and images of the truth about life and your future.

This guide book can help you to abandon the wounds of your past and find self-love and self-worth and help you to live the "meassage" that is your authentic journey, graduation, and commencement and not the one imposed upon you by the words and actions of abusive authority figures. The opposite of love is indifference, rejection, and abuse—all of which you can eliminate from your life by using the guidance of this wonderful book of wisdom. When you live in your heart, magic happens.

So read on, and become what I call a LOVE WARRIOR. From here on in your life, love will be your weapon of choice, and you will see the difference it makes in your life as well as the lives of others. People don't know what to do with you when your weapon is love, and you will notice how often people contact you when they miss your love and its nourishing effect.

Bernie Siegel, MD

Bestselling author of *The Art of Healing, 365 Prescriptions For The Soul* and *Love, Medicine & Miracles*, named one of the top 20 Spiritually Influential Living People on the Planet by the *Watkins Review*.

Unconventional Conventions

Notes on the Text

INSPIRATION

THE READER WILL SEE AT THE END of some of the sections and activities in this workbook the use of the word "Inspiration" followed by a superscript number, much the same as referencing an explanatory note or a resource in a bibliography. The word "Inspiration" is a signal for the reader to see the attached "Notes and Credits" section at the back of this workbook for more information.

The choice of the word "Inspiration" is two-fold. First, it gives additional acknowledgement to the people and concepts that have inspired portions of the text. Second, it intentionally breaks from convention. Often traditional conventions are meaningless in the sense of who we are as people, as human beings, especially in the area of internal work. The exploration and work that are experienced by a student in the study of Tai Chi is just that, internal work. This internal work is the path one travels to get back to one's "authentic self," the point of studying Tai Chi, meditation, and mindfulness.

ITALICS

The use of italics in the text is to make note of a quote. Italics are also used to signal and identify words written in Pinyin, which is the official phonetic system for the pronunciations of Chinese characters, and to transliterate these characters into the Latin alphabet. Chinese is the language of origin of Tai Chi and was the vehicle in the original transmission and sharing of this art.

In addition, I took the liberty of breaking convention by italicizing the words *Ch'i Essential* or *Ch'i Essentials* as a special designation of the mindfulness activities contained within this workbook.

CAPITALIZATION

Another break from traditional convention is the capitalization of certain words in the text. This is done intentionally to call special attention to a word and/or as a sign of respect.

For example, the capitalization of the word "Grandmaster" is used to respect and honor the accomplishments of many of my teachers who have dedicated their lives to studying and sharing Tai Chi. They were all senior representatives and students of Professor Cheng Man-Ching, the person responsible for bringing Tai Chi (Taiji) to the United States and Europe. These Grandmasters reflect in their teachings the special flavor Professor (as he was fondly called) brought to this fine art.

The word "Spirit" is capitalized to denote a larger perspective, something that is beyond merely a thought. This is a special use in the text to point the reader in the right direction of understanding, emphasizing an air of importance or sacredness. Spirit is different for each of us. For some, it represents the "Divine" (a similar use of capitalization), or one's "Higher Power," or the "One," or "God."

In addition, "Reflection Journal" is capitalized to reference the journal that readers keep as they progress with their mindfulness activities or *Ch'i Essentials*.

The words "Tai Chi Principle" are capitalized along with the name of a specific principle so it will stand out in importance from the rest of the text.

Form is another example of strategic capitalization. Form is capitalized to draw attention to an additional way this Tai Chi exercise is referenced. People often say, "Let's do a round of Form." The word "round," in this case, means going through the entire choreography once.

Flow is capitalized so its importance is emphasized. Tai Chi promotes Flow as well as *ch'i* flow. Everything works better in life when you are in a state of Flow. Flow is an example of "Effortless Effort."

TRUTH

*"The mind is like a parachute.
It doesn't work unless it's open."*

FRANK ZAPPA

Introduction

TAI CHI, OR MORE PROPERLY T'ai Chi Ch'uan, is mostly known as a slow moving meditation. There is a "Form," a choreography, that a person learns and practices. But to me, and many of the teachers I've studied under, simply learning the movements is not the point of the exercise. Instead, a form is just that, a framework. It is an empty vessel that one learns to fill when practicing Tai Chi.

The way the form becomes something more than an empty framework, creating something beautiful and meaningful, is when the mind and *ch'i*, ones life energy (often referred to as universal energy) are engaged and added to the equation. Mindful awareness, that is, an alert and relaxed presence, and *ch'i*, are what makes this art Tai Chi. Without it, the exercise is simply calisthenics.

Ben Lo, one of the great Grandmasters of the Cheng Man-Ching lineage, would often explain in class that we study and use the Form as a place to practice the Tai Chi principles. And this is the point of the exercise, to learn, practice, explore and internalize the Tai Chi principles.

At some point in time, students begin to realize that they are practicing these Tai Chi principles all day long in everything that they do. This is what I call one of Tai Chi's little enlightenments. Everything begins to change. The use of your mind, your mindful awareness and your *ch'i*, now become essential to your journey through life. Everything starts to become more delicious. It can be described as the joy of doing whatever you are doing in the moment, the here and now. And this points to the Principle of Flow. When you are in balance and in harmony with people, events and all the situations around you, everything works better.

Tai Chi and the Art of Mindfulness is designed as a workbook for my students at West Chester University where I share this wonderful art as part of a minor degree program, which the University offers in Contemplative Studies. However, anyone interested in self-improvement or self-cultivation can benefit from the exercises and activities contained in this workbook. They are called *Ch'i Essentials*.

The *Ch'i Essentials* focus on cultivating mindfulness and mindful awareness in one's daily life. In addition, they help build your energy and personal power, a necessity to creating a sustainable state of Flow in your life. The *Ch'i Essentials* are tied to the Tai Chi principles and how one can practice and live these principles all day long. The concept of Nei Gong (pronounced *nay gong*) means "Inner Work." It is precisely these internal *Ch'i Essential* activities that raise your consciousness, creating a fertile environment for spiritual growth and for what Abraham Maslow calls self-actualization. Maslow stressed the importance of focusing on the positive qualities in people.[1] In addition, Tai Chi and these *Ch'i Essentials* help expand your possibilities as you learn to maximize and reach your highest potential.

I invite anyone using this workbook to do the *Ch'i Essentials* contained within. I recommend that you keep a journal as a record of your progress and growth. Go back from time to time and read your entries. You will be pleasantly surprised by what you find.

At the end of each semester, when we meet for our final class, I enjoy explaining to the students that if they have gained anything from the course and their study of Tai Chi, that it is all due to their work. Tai Chi and its mindfulness, what Professor Cheng Man-Ching calls "self-cultivation," is at its heart an internal art. I, or for that matter any other instructor, cannot get inside students and do the work for them. Anything gained from its study is solely due to all the good work that students do themselves.

Enjoy this book and the gifts within. Play. And with the heart of an explorer on an inner journey, embrace all your opportunities to celebrate another day in our global village, our home, this bountiful planet we call Earth.

How To Use
This Workbook

PART ONE

LOVE

Reflection and Insight Journal

HOW TO APPROACH THE *CH'I ESSENTIALS*

TAI CHI AND ITS MINDFULNESS is an art that can only be understood and learned through experience. As a contemplative study, you need to allow yourself not only to have an experience, but to feel it in your body and then think about it. Grandmaster Maggie Newman often reminds us in class, "You should always go back to: *What am I feeling in my body?*" Whether you are playing Push Hands or just shifting your weight, Maggie says, "It's a feeling thing . . . a feeling of love."

Chade-Meng Tan, the head of personal growth at Google, offers the following insight. "Contemplative practices can help people succeed in life and work. They can be beneficial to people's careers and to business bottom lines."[1]

Next, comes reflection and insights. One of the best ways to reflect is through journaling. Use your journal to consider what your experiences with the various *Ch'i Essential* activities mean and how they can benefit you in your daily life.

Tai Chi is an activity of mind. Without the mind, it is not Tai Chi. Each reflection should demonstrate that your mind is engaged, that you are considering the importance of what you experienced and took some time to figure out what it means to you. This is an opportunity to connect the

dots in new ways, consider new and many powerful ancient ideas, as well as develop a wisdom and a point of view that honors you and your Spirit.

The point of the Reflection and Insight Journal is for your mind to engage again in the process, which promotes your inner growth. This is the Tai Chi part. Consider the possibilities of how each *Ch'i Essential* activity can impact your journey and your day-to-day activities, as well as your consciousness. Writing down your thoughts promotes clarity and mindfulness.

REFLECTIVE JOURNALING QUESTIONS

Below is a list of general questions that will aid in your reflective journaling. The entire list will not be pertinent to all the *Ch'i Essentials*, but many will act as a thoughtful guide to your inquiry.

1. What was the point of the *Ch'i Essential* activity?

2. What did you experience?

3. How did it make you feel?

4. What does the experience you had with each *Ch'i Essential* activity mean to you?

5. How can the *Ch'i Essential* help your practice of Tai Chi's mindfulness?

6. How can what you experienced impact your daily life?

7. What did you learn or at least consider?

8. What did you learn about yourself?

9. What did the experience you had with the *Ch'i Essential* do to help reduce your stress?

    Was your level of anxiety lowered?

    Did the amount that you worry lessen?

Remember, these *Ch'i Essentials* are designed for you, to help you consider new possibilities that can improve your journey through life, create more enjoyment and happiness, as well as the ability to contribute more to the world around you. These are your opportunities to discover your own personal truths, ideas, and beliefs that support you moving toward your dreams and desires. This is an opportunity to focus on yourself, and this is the self-cultivation that Tai Chi offers. You get to discover and awaken your authentic self and the special gifts you bring to the world.

REFLECTIVE JOURNALING QUESTIONS

10. How did the *Ch'i Essential* activity impact your energy?

    What did it do to your attitude?

    Has your daily Flow increased?

    What else did you notice?

11. What changes do you notice in your daily life?

    Are you sleeping better?

    Getting fewer colds and headaches?

    Are you more "present"?

    Do you notice the absence of negative thoughts, a.k.a. the Monkey Mind?

    Are you enjoying your day more?

    Are your grades or work product improving?

    Are your relationships improving and becoming more fulfilling?

12. If other people were involved in the *Ch'i Essential* activity, what did you notice about their energy?

    What did you notice about their experience?

    How did the *Ch'i Essential* impact their attitude?

DREAM

Evidence Journal

TAI CHI TEACHES THAT WHAT you focus on and how you focus really makes a difference in your life. You use *Xin Yi*. *Xin* means heart, and *Yi* means mind; together they create the heart-mind. In Western culture, the heart-mind is best understood as an intention. The initial intention a student focuses on is nurturing.[1] You start with setting an intention and then you add your attention. This is what makes it Tai Chi—the simultaneous use of your mind and consciousness. Your mind is relaxed and alert at the same time. As in any creative process, thought must precede form. This is intention.

As you investigate this wonderful process of self-cultivation, you get to focus on your dreams and desires in life. And what could be better? Then you get to see how your dreams and desires begin to show up and become fulfilled. You start to see evidence that the universe is supporting your journey.

Let's change gears for a moment. Did you ever have the feeling of interconnectedness? To nature? To a girlfriend, boyfriend, or parent? Maybe you felt this interconnectedness when you were sitting on a beach with your significant other watching a sunset. Tai Chi helps you to feel the interconnection of all things as well as the inner connection of everything in your internal environment. You begin by bringing the mind and body together to create unity or mind-body. Then you marry the environment, and at the highest level of self-cultivation, the Spirit is engaged. This is *Shen* energy. Tai Chi is the study of the Tao, and the Tao is a study of being in harmony and balance with all that is.

"Pay attention to nurturing. Every Taiji exercise should be done with this intention."

DR. YANG YANG

"Relation and connection are not somewhere and sometime, but everywhere and always."

EMERSON

Do you believe in synchronicities, coincidences, and chance encounters? These are wonderful ideas that are often misconstrued. For example, most people think that a coincident is an accident, a fluke or random event. However, mathematics refers to coincident as things that fit together perfectly, like coincidental angles. The dictionary definition of coincident is 1) "occurring together in space or time." Again we see it refers to things that go together. And 2) "in agreement or harmony," a concept similar to what the Tao teaches.

Eckhart Tolle, a prominent spiritual leader whom *Watkins Review* listed as the most spiritually influential person in the world, said:[2]

> *"When you become a conscious part of the interconnectedness of the whole and its purpose: the emergence of consciousness into this world . . . spontaneous helpful occurrences, chance encounters, coincidences, and synchronistic events happen much more frequently."*

The Evidence Journal is a special kind of reflection journal. It can help support your journey toward your dreams and desires. The insights you glean come from a greater awareness, a more focused approach to paying attention to your life. These reflective essays you create through journaling are part of documenting your exploration of Tai Chi. As your consciousness awakens and changes as a result of playing with Tai Chi's principles, ideas, philosophies and mindfulness, you will experience the "spontaneous helpful occurrences" that Mr. Tolle mentioned. This journal is the place to make note of what is showing up to support your journey toward what you desire most in life. It is a record of your progress. Read it from time to time and notice how it makes you feel.

Remember synchronicities, coincidences, and chance encounters might not be exactly what they initially appear to be. Whatever you experience, whether it's out in the world or a little nudge in your gut, do not judge it. Just note in your Evidence Journal. Your journal will help you learn how to pay attention in a different way. For example, upon reading your entries three or four months down the road, you can identify a pattern that supports you and a deeper understanding of your progress can occur. You are testing, exploring and investigating. It is a process of self-cultivation

"Coincidences are God's way of remaining anonymous."

ALBERT EINSTEIN

"Quiet your mind, listen for the voice, do what feels right, look for signs to direct you, and watch how the coincidences and miracles start to happen."

DR. BERNIE SIEGEL
MIND-BODY EXPERT

that you study. Taoism suggests that the destination is the journey. Use your journal to engage your mind and your inner nature. This is the heart-mind, and within the heart-mind is where the magic happens.

> *"Man's mind, once stretched by a new idea,*
> *never regains its original dimensions."*
>
> FORTUNE COOKIE

AMBITION

Ch'i Essentials
Mindfulness Activities

PART TWO

德

VIRTUE

"Nonsense wakes up the brain cells. And it helps develop a sense of humor, which is awfully important in this day and age. Humor has a tremendous place in this sordid world. It's more than just a matter of laughing. If you can see things out of whack, then you can see how things can be in whack."

DR. SEUSS

Clean Joke

PEOPLE WHO DO TAI CHI are known as Tai Chi Players. It's fun when you play. We play music, we have playgrounds in parks and at schools, and there are a myriad of other ways in which we engage in play. Play lifts and fills the heart. It recharges and energizes the Spirit. How can you start to incorporate more fun and more play into your daily life?

More opportunities exist for play than you might realize. How do you feel addressing a room full of people? Do you get nervous or a little scared? Telling a joke is an excellent opportunity to practice the Tai Chi Principle of Rooting and feel less anxious. Developing a root, a connection to the ground, to the Earth, is how we do Tai Chi. All the movements are driven from the ground up. When you feel solid on your feet, you can relax and let go of tension. When you feel solid on your feet and truly connected to the Earth, you can think clearer and make better decisions.

Over the next week, take at least three opportunities to share a Clean Joke. Share a joke with a group of coworkers or friends. How about with a group of strangers in the checkout line at your local supermarket? If you're really courageous, how about with people in an elevator? That's what I call a captive audience. Remember to feel your feet on the floor, put a smile on your face, and go for it. How much play can you bring into the world? When you mindfully bring play into the world, you begin to experience the Tai Chi Principle of Flow in your life.

Here's a suggestion. Download a few jokes so you have them to play with and share with others. Plus they're fun!

A horse walks into a bar . . .

"Adults are just obsolete children and the hell with them."

DR. SEUSS

"When I let go of what I am, I become what I might be."

LAO TZU
TAO TE CHING

The Tao
The Way

THE TAO, LITERALLY TRANSLATED, means "The Way," or "The Path." The *Tao Te Ching* is one of the oldest written books, dating back to the 6th century BCE. It was written by the sage Lao Tzu. Lao Tzu means "Old Master." Think of Lao Tzu as the original Mr. Miyagi from the film *The Karate Kid.*

The *Tao Te Ching* has many suggestions for a way to be in the world, in your life, with your family and friends, in your work and contributions, and the like. Both Tai Chi's and the *Tao Te Ching*'s focus is on self-cultivation, which results in learning how to be a Master in your own life.

The full translation of the *Tao Te Ching* is this: *Tao* means "The Way." *Te* means "Virtue," "Personal Character," "Inner Strength" (Virtuosity), or "Integrity." *Ching* means "Great Book," or "Classic." Put together we have "The Classic of the Way (Path) and the Power/Virtue."[1]

For this *Ch'i Essential* find out one thing that the Tao has to offer that honors you as well as your practice of mindfulness as you move toward being a Master in your own life. The Tao needs interpretation to fully understand its wisdom and how to apply it to your journey. What is your interpretation? What does it mean to you?

Meditation is "the next new frontier of human exploration."

JEFF WARREN, FOUNDER, THE CONSCIOUSNESS EXPLORERS CLUB

清

CLARITY

You In Six Words

TELL YOUR LIFE STORY IN SIX WORDS

THIS *CH'I ESSENTIAL* WAS INSPIRED by Ernest Hemingway's shortest of all short stories. It's a quick read, enjoy.

> *"For sale: Baby shoes, never worn."*

Write your life story using only six words. Hemingway wrote his six-word story long before there was Twitter.

There is inspiration everywhere. Even if you don't think you're a story-teller, you are. You don't even have to write a complete sentence. How does your life look in six words?

> *"Inspiration is the greatest gift because it opens your life to*
> *many new possibilities. Each day becomes more meaningful,*
> *and your life is enhanced when your actions are guided*
> *by what inspires you."*
>
> DR. BERNIE SIEGEL
> MIND-BODY EXPERT

Professor Cheng Man-Ching is one of the greatest Tai Chi Masters of all time. He is the teacher of several of the masters I've had the privilege of studying under. This is his life story in six words:

> *"Loving kindness and passion for self-mastery."*

Tai Chi is about self-cultivation and self-discovery. As an experiment, you will take a look at the result of your exploration of the mindfulness Tai Chi has to offer the world. After you have completed the exercises in this book, you will repeat this *Ch'i Essential* without looking back on the six-word life story you write today. Then the fun and opportunity for insights begins when you compare both versions of your life story to see what you can discover.

Inspiration[1]

SIX WORD LIFE STORIES

Here are some examples of life stories to get your brain fired up:

1. Might as well eat that cookie. (Famous Chef)
2. Include everyone. Be kind. Have fun.
3. Loving heart for sale. Like new.
4. I have time to fix this.
5. Stage IV cancer made me live.
6. Sorry I'm not married yet, Mom.
7. I've made all the best mistakes.
8. Car totaled. Lives spared. Forever grateful.
9. Sharing love, light, joy. Empowering everyone.
10. I raised a United States Marine.
11. Best move ever? I married her.
12. Still fit into high school earrings.
13. I have Asperger's, what's your excuse.
14. Carjacked in the tunnel of love.

Highest Happiness

THE HAPPY ONE

WHO SAID, "GO FOR THE HIGHEST HAPPINESS?"

This person was known as "The Happy One."

Why do you think this person suggested this?

What do you think they meant?

What does it mean to you?

Why go for the highest happiness?

Why not go for the highest success?

Or go for the highest contribution?

How can this wisdom and insight help your exploration
of mindfulness through the Tai Chi principles?

信任

TRUST

"It's not that things are right in my life that I am happy;
it's that I'm happy that things are right in my life."

What Brings You Joy?

TAI CHI CAN INFORM EVERY area of your life, however a word of caution is in order. Just like I let my students know at the beginning of each semester, I want to inform you, the reader, as well. There's an inevitable side effect from the exploration of Tai Chi and the mindfulness it offers, and that is happiness and joy.

Fortunately for most of us, we welcome joy into our hearts with open arms. However, the subject bears further scrutiny.

Joy is often different for each of us, and it can flow into our lives in various ways. But when a key ingredient is added, joy can instantly become more accessible. In fact, we can then become an active participant in experiencing more joy in our daily activities and begin to make choices that move us toward increasing our joy. This special ingredient, or the secret sauce as they say, is "mindfulness." Mindful awareness helps to keep the opportunities for experiencing joy alive in our consciousness.

For this Ch'i Essential you are going to answer the question: "What brings you joy?" Even though the question appears simple at first glance, finding an answer can often be elusive.

I suggest you start by asking yourself, "What do I like to do?" and then ask, "Why?" This questioning begins a process of discovery. Think about the question for a while, and then be as specific as you can in your answer. Most people come to the conclusion that the reason they like to do something is because it makes them "feel good." This conclusion is the perfect start, taking things to a feeling level. One of the goals of

Tai Chi is to get back to your authentic self, and a component of that is trusting and connecting to how things feel inside.

Now you are ready to really explore, "What brings you joy?" Consider the question and for all answers that you bring up, continue asking, "Why?" This process will move you toward the root of what brings joy for you. Continue to drill down and repeatedly ask yourself "Why?" Notice the more times you can answer "why," the lighter and happier you begin to feel.

Joy is not a goal. The word "goal" tends to imply that once something is achieved, that is it's end, which is not what one wants when trying to obtain or find joy in his or her life. Rather than a goal, joy is part of the process of self-cultivation. Sustainable joy becomes possible when you practice the element of mindfulness in all that you engage. Is there joy in what you're doing? You can and will create that state by being present in all the small steps you take on your way toward any larger goal. Being ever-present is one way you can obtain high energy without stress, no matter what goal is your focus.

A wonderful benefit of answering the question, "What brings you joy," is the ability to recognize the opportunities that lead to joy when they show up.

When you are mindfully aware of what brings you joy, you can then embrace the power of choices. You can actively choose to engage in more of the interests, activities, environments, and people that contribute to your joy. You then can create experiences that empower you.

What new ideas and thoughts about joy did you discover? What did you learn that could promote more joy and more Flow in your life?

In finding answers that work for you, your mind and heart had to engage in the process. *Xin Yi*, or the heart-mind, is an intention. Set the intention to continue discovering more and more joy in all that you do. Notice what shows up!

6

Conscious Breath

PART A

BREATHING IS OUR ONLY NATURAL, ongoing exchange with our environment. Breathing is also one of the best ways to practice mindful awareness because your breath brings oxygen to your brain and body, creating a sense of calm.[1] The breath connects the mind and body, creating unity.

"Breathe in the *ch'i* of heaven to become resilient as an infant," was Professor Cheng Man-Ching's basic advice for the study of Tai Chi. Air is the foundation for all *ch'i* development.[2]

The Conscious Breath is a special kind of breath. It is one that you feel and listen to with all of your senses. Inhale deep into your abdomen. This is your *Dan Tien*, your energy center. Translated it means "Sea of *Ch'i*." It is infinitely deep, like an ocean. As you inhale, feel the breath extend to your fingertips and toes. Feel the expansion of your lungs as the air fills them.

Each inhalation, filling the lungs from the bottom up, is an energizing event, charging the body. Each exhalation is a release, a letting go.[1] Feel your body let go and relax as the air gently leaves. Tension just floats away.

The Conscious Breath helps us to find the stillness that is already there inside of us.[3] With this technique, you relax the mind and prepare it to function better, removing stress and anxiety.

There is a remarkable phenomenon that happens when you take a Conscious Breath. You simply cannot hold a thought in your head. You cannot

"Breathe in the ch'i of heaven to become resilient as an infant."

CHENG MAN-CHING

think and be aware of your breathing at the same time. The Conscious Breath stops your mind for a nanosecond, creating a little gap of stillness.

Test the Conscious Breath. Try and hold a thought in your mind, and then inhale and feel the breath with all of your senses. Notice the gap where one thought ends and the next one begins. The more you practice the Conscious Breath, the duration of the gap increases. You become free of mind identification, that little voice in your head. There is less thinking and more mind—the cultivation of mindfulness. You are just there, present, experiencing the world.

Your *Ch'i Essential* activity uses this wonderful technology to still the mind with a touchstone. A touchstone is an object that you touch to remind you of something, in this case, to breathe. It helps to create mindful awareness without effort. Your touchstone can be any object of your choosing, like your smartphone, or your car keys, or even the handle to your refrigerator. Choose an object that you will touch at least three times a day.

For the next week, every time you touch your touchstone, think "*Relax*" and take a Conscious Breath. You only need to take three Conscious Breaths a day, but feel free to take more.

Toward the end of the week, notice how different you feel. Notice if that gap of stillness is increasing. Begin to notice the lack of tension or any decrease in your level of stress. In fact, if you find yourself in a high-pressure situation, like facing a crucial deadline or having a difficult conversation at home or work, stop and take a Conscious Breath. It will only take you a second. Then notice the difference.

Here is a playful idea. A student decided to create a visual touchstone and put stickers on objects she would see during her day, like the Apple on her computer. She placed stickers on her book bag, on her bathroom mirror, and so forth to use as a reminder to take a Conscious Breath.

Another student, who became very tense when driving, used a traffic light as her visual touchstone. She created what she called her "Red Light Meditation." Whenever she came to a red light, she would put her car into park, drop her hands into her lap, and even close her eyes. She then took several Conscious Breaths. In addition to being more relaxed when driving, she noticed how friendly and helpful people were. The person behind her would always let her know when the light had changed from red to green. Remember, safety first in all situations.[4]

呼
吸

BREATHE

Conscious Breath

PART B

HOW OFTEN DO YOU WAKE UP in the morning and start thinking about your day? Your mind immediately engages in all you have to do, where you have to go, as well as the people you need to interact with and the activities you have to participate in. Your eyes are barely open, yet your mind and consciousness have run ahead and are a million miles away from your bedroom, jitterbugging all over the place.

And how about in the shower? Here too, a person's mind begins to think about all the people they'll need to interact with, their boss, clients, colleagues, and then, *BLAM!* There they are. All those folks are right there in the shower with them—at least in their mind. The person's mind has leaped beyond the present to focus on the future. As a result, many people do not even feel the warmth of the water or the slipperiness of the soap on their skin. In short, Elvis has left the shower!

A great way to practice mindfulness and mindful awareness is to stop, wait a moment, and practice the Principle of Slowing Down.

For Part B of this *Ch'i Essential*, you are to extend the Conscious Breath for a second week. Here's a suggestion to get you started and refocus your morning: Take your first of three Conscious Breaths of the day right after you wake up. Just lie there in your bed and feel your breath go down, deep into your abdomen as you gently inhale. Feel the warmth of the sheets and the comfort of the covers all around you. Exhale slowly and give yourself permission to simply lie there and connect to your body

and your environment for at least five seconds. That's it. Then, after that, feel free to get up and go to crazy-town if you must. You can let your mind rush into your day ahead of you if you want, but please take the five seconds as a special gift just for you. Give it to yourself.

REFLECTION AND INSIGHT JOURNAL TIPS

Write a second reflection at the end of the week. Here are a few additional questions to deepen your inquiry.

1. What has changed and what do you notice that is different from week one to week two as you continue to deepen your mindful practice with the Conscious Breath?

2. Do you notice any difference in how you feel?

3. Is that gap of stillness expanding even more?

4. Do you have more energy?

5. Do you notice that your day-to-day tension is floating away faster?

6. Continue to explore what happens when you take three Conscious Breaths each day.

Standing

YOUR CONNECTION TO THE EARTH is your root. Rooting is one of the five fundamental skills in Tai Chi. You root through your feet, your only connection to the planet unless you are sitting or lying down.

Most people already know how to put their minds into their hands. That's easy. It's something you do every day when reaching into a dark room to flip on a light switch, or when you reach out to turn off the alarm clock before your eyes are open.

In order to root, you need to learn how to put your mind into your feet. Few people think about this. Tai Chi trains you to feel the ground beneath your feet. Imagine stepping your foot and resting it on the ground without any weight in it, an empty step. But what about your other foot? If one foot is empty, the other foot is full. It has all your weight in it. This is a manifestation of Yin and Yang, the separation of empty and full in the legs. Now imagine stepping the foot and having the sensitivity to feel an ant underneath it and not crush the little guy. This is Tai Chi sensitivity training.

When the foot is full, you learn to think down, deep into the center of the Earth, and feel the connection. This is rooting. Up to three-quarters of a tree's size is underground in its roots. The Tao teaches that we can learn a lot from nature.

You also learn to focus on the internal alignment of your body. Tai Chi teaches that the balance point for the body, the place where you can reach central equilibrium, is to have the weight fall under the ankles. This is

"Walk as if you are kissing the Earth with your feet."

THICH NHAT HANH
PEACE IS EVERY STEP

the place where there is the least stress and physical tension on your body, while you are still maintaining an upright posture. In essence, you create a new homeostasis or a new neutral position for your spine through Tai Chi alignment.

The body's nerves, which are connected to all of your organs, communicate to the brain. Most are connected through your spinal cord. In essence, this is your central nervous system, which is defined as the brain and spinal cord. The central nervous system controls almost everything you do, from walking and talking, to the things your body does for you automatically, like breathing and digesting your food. This complex system is also involved with your five senses, seeing, hearing, touching, tasting, and smelling, as well as things like your emotions, thoughts, and memory.[1]

The improved spinal alignment Tai Chi creates also helps with your brain health, including the pumping of your cerebral spinal fluid and your blood, which delivers oxygen and other nutrients to nourish your brain.

If you look at a skeleton, you can see that the balance point is the bump at the back of the head, the tailbone, and the ankles. When the weight falls under the ankles, it will spread out evenly across the entire footprint, enhancing your root. Spreading the weight out evenly across the entire footprint is what is desired in Tai Chi.

Check the wear patterns on your old shoes or sneakers. Do you notice the inner or outer edge around the toes to be more worn out on one side or the other? How about around the heel? For this *Ch'i Essential*, change how you stand. Redistribute your weight to compensate for the wear patterns. Don't worry. You cannot overcorrect. Remember to keep your knees unlocked, even when your legs are straight. Locked knees will create tension in the joints and has the potential to cause a state of collapse. Allow your head to float up and chin to relax down as you continue to mindfully redistribute your weight.

Do this *Ch'i Essential* for one week. Notice how it feels to have less stress and tension from gravity acting on your body. Do you notice any other areas of your body letting go and relaxing? Often, there is tension in other parts of the body that you are unaware of. This is because additional muscles must be used to compensate for how you stand to keep you vertical when the weight does not fall under the ankles. You are now creating a habit where those muscles get to relax, release and let go, plus you are honoring your physiology.

GRACE

An Amazing Life

PART A

HOW WOULD YOU LIKE TO be living an amazing life? Of course you would. Everybody wants to. So what does living an amazing life look like for you? It is different for everyone. When can you honestly say you are living an amazing life?

Think about how amazing your life could be. Think about what rules and criteria you need to fulfill to say that you are living an amazing life. What do you need to accomplish? What needs to happen so that you feel your life is really amazing?

1. Do you need straight 'A's?

2. How about graduating?

3. Do you need that special job,
    the one paying a salary in the high six figures,
    to think that you are living an amazing life?

4. How about when you find that perfect mate?
    Will your life be truly amazing then?

5. How about that beach house? Or the cottage in the mountains? Is that part of your picture of what living an amazing life looks like?

Ask yourself this: What is having a truly amazing life dependent on? What ducks do you need to get in a row for your life to appear absolutely amazing to you?

For this *Ch'i Essential*, write out your description. Be specific and put in as much detail as you can imagine. You'll want to know what living an amazing life looks like, so that when it shows up, you'll recognize it.

The 29 Gifts

29 DAYS OF CONSCIOUS GIVING AND MOVING ENERGY

THE 29 GIFTS *CH'I ESSENTIAL* is an experiment to see if you can change your life in a month with very little effort and, at the same time, move a lot of positive energy out into the world. This is another example of the "Do Less – Achieve More" philosophy.

Albert Einstein said:

> *"There are only two ways to live your life. One is as though nothing is a miracle. The other is as though everything is a miracle."*

Whichever way you choose to live your life and to believe in, this is an activity of the heart-mind. It will change the way you experience everything in the world.

FIRST QUESTION

Let's begin with the question, "What would you do if your world fell apart?" You woke up and everything is changed. Forget going back to work or school. Forget participating in sports or even hanging out with your friends anymore.

How would you respond if you woke up with a debilitating illness? This is an illness where every day you experience excruciating pain in your neck and back, have weakness in your limbs, your arms and legs. Next

add hypersensitivity to the gentlest touch, where even the lightness of the clothes you wear causes irritation and pain all over your body. Add to that a skewed sense of balance, and some serious cognitive problems. Now throw in the curve ball of emotional and self-esteem issues that result from these problems. Oh, and there's one more thing. There is no cure!

This is Cami Walker's story, a young woman who got married, went on her honeymoon, and a month later was diagnosed with Multiple Sclerosis, a chronic and progressive disease of the central nervous system. Can you imagine what she went through and what she felt? Finding the man of her dreams, having a promising career, and then it's all over in the blink of an eye.

"The most powerful tool in the doctor's "little black bag" to prevent or treat illness is the patient's (your) own mind!"

DR. BERNIE SIEGEL
MIND-BODY EXPERT

After running out of options with traditional western medicine, Cami Walker finally found Mbali Creazzo, a South African Medicine Woman who works at the Center for Health and Healing at California Pacific Hospital. She gave Cami a solution and an untraditional prescription.

Mbali said to Cami, *"Stop thinking about yourself.* If you spend all your time and energy focusing on your pain, you're feeding it. You're making it worse by putting all of your attention there."

Can you imagine what went through Cami's mind when she heard this directive, "Stop thinking about yourself?" Here is a young woman in pain; all her daily activities have been replaced by doctors' visits and research into what is available for an MS patient. How can you think of anything else when you're in that situation and your life has abruptly changed forever?

But Mbali did not stop there. She went on to say, "Healing doesn't happen in a vacuum, but through our interactions with other people. By giving, you are focusing on what you have to offer others, inviting more abundance into your life."

Ms. Creazzo then instructed Cami to give away "29 Gifts in 29 Days." For this *Ch'i Essential*, you are going to experience and take Cami's untraditional prescription. If this activity changed Cami Walker's life in 29 days, imagine what it can do for you, someone who is healthy and active, and not challenged by the severe medical conditions surrounding a life debilitating illness?

Remember, the use of the mind, or more specifically, *Xin Yi*, the heart-mind, is the active ingredient in Tai Chi.

SECOND QUESTION

Are you focused on yourself and your work? On getting ahead in your career or getting good grades and doing the best you can to prepare for a life with more opportunities in your future? To do this *Ch'i Essential* activity, you'll have to change your focus and create a new type of mindful awareness. You will now need to focus on other people, not on yourself.

SIX SECRETS TO GIVING

1. START WITH GRATITUDE
    Write down what you are most thankful for and make a point to share at least one item on your list.

2. KEEP IT SIMPLE
    Small gestures often make the biggest impact. Smile at a stranger, offer a coworker a sincere compliment, or buy someone lunch for no reason. Hold a door for someone and be generous with your smile.

3. GIVE UP EXPECTATIONS
    Let go of judgements. This is a Taoist philosophy and a Tai Chi Principle. Let go and do not judge how your gift will be received or put to use. Once you have given it, your gift will take care of itself. Do not expect a gift or even an acknowledgment of your giving a gift in return. Just put your positive energy, *ch'i*, out into the world.

    Lao Tzu, in the *Tao Te Ching*, talks about how the sage creates great change:

    > *"The sage does not take credit for anything. Do lots of little things to create a great change."*

"We can only be said to be alive in those moments when our hearts are conscious of our treasures."

THORNTON WILDER[a]

a   Thornton Wilder is a playwright, novelist, and winner of three Pulitzer Prizes

4.   RECEIVE GRACIOUSLY

This is an opportunity to balance energy, to experience the continual flow of Yin and Yang. Giving without receiving will deplete your energy. Remember to be receptive to what others are eager to share with you. Notice that the gifts that come into your

"You give but little when you give of your possessions. It is when you give of yourself that you truly give."

KHALIL GIBRAN[a]

EXAMPLES OF GIVING

Use these examples as a guide to your mindful gift-giving.

1.   Offer a kind word or thought, instead of keeping quiet.

2.   Call a friend who is struggling and give them some kind words.

3.   Put a couple of dollars in the church collection basket.

4.   Bring food to a sick or hungry person, or make someone a meal.

5.   Take old sweaters or unused clothing to Goodwill.

6.   Fill a friend's parking meter.

7.   Send a box of tea to your mother.

8.   Call Mom and Dad. Tell them you just wanted to hear their voice, and tell them that you love them. This is a huge gift to any parent.

9.   Give someone flowers.

10. Send positive energy through prayers and meditation.

11. Listen to a friend.

12. Bring a friend a book.

13. Say "Thank You," expressing sincere gratitude.

14. Offer a coworker or fellow student a sincere compliment.

15. Smile at a stranger.

16. Write someone a nice note.

a   Khalil Gibran, author of *The Prophet* (1923), a book of 26 poetic essays; a must read for inspiration. Gibran is also a well-known Arab poet, writer, artist, and philosopher.

life will most likely come from a different source than the recipients of your gifts. Could this be another example of the interconnectedness of all things?

5. WING IT

Resist the urge to plan all 29 Gifts in one sitting. Stay open to the gift-giving opportunities that occur naturally throughout any given day. Stay present and be in the moment. Be conscious of all your daily opportunities to move energy and lift people.

6. CHALLENGE YOURSELF

This is an optional suggestion for giving, a special opportunity, one that requires a little more mindful digging within. Ask yourself: What are you hesitant to give? Your time? Unconditional love? Then ask yourself "why" and try to let those hang-ups go. Mbali suggested to Cami to give as a gift "at least one thing you think you can't live without."

Giving is sharing energy. How we cultivate and use energy is a focus in the Art of Tai Chi and its mindfulness. As you do these 29 Gifts *Ch'i Essential* activities, is life getting better? Is life becoming more alive for you? Notice how you feel.

What can you give of yourself to another person? Here is a wonderful opportunity to practice "Without Effort" in your daily life. Give without effort. Just let it happen. Give with joy and be open to receive joy. When you give from the heart, the heart fills. This is balance. It's Yin-Yang. And it's moving energy.

Most of you are probably already giving gifts like these every day, but with the 29 Gifts *Ch'i Essential* we add an additional element, and that is your consciousness, your mindful awareness. Notice where your intentions go in your gift-giving. This is *Xin Yi*, the use of the heart-mind. This is another way to practice the Tai Chi Principles in your day-to-day life.

Upon completion of Cami Walker's 29 Gifts prescription, Mbali said to her, "You did something very brave. It's a profound moment in all of our lives when we can let go of control and surrender to something bigger."

Take a look at these wonderful examples Cami Walker shares of using *ch'i*, her personal energy:

"My value isn't measured by how much I accomplish, and the limitations that MS imposes on my body do not stop me from living a purposeful life. I have the power to touch other people and move them to action."

CAMI WALKER

"The simplest of gifts often carry the most meaning: small gestures that show people you care."

CAMI WALKER

Letting go and surrendering is perfect Tai Chi. It is a very difficult lesson to learn and to practice. This is the yielding part of Tai Chi. This is honoring the Yin in life.

This is what Cami does everyday, in her own words: "I pray and spend at least a few minutes in meditative reflection. I give at least one gift to another person whose path I'm blessed to cross. And I say thank you as many times as I can."

> *"Giving is more joyous than receiving, not because it is deprivation, but because in the act of giving lies the expression of my aliveness."*

ERICH FROMM[a]

REFLECTION AND INSIGHT JOURNAL TIPS

Notice where you direct your intentions. Notice what happens to your day-to-day gratitude. Are you becoming more aware of the gifts and blessing in your life, the things you have to be grateful for each day?

What insights do you have on your new focus of giving? During the 29 days, take some notes. Jot down any insights that you experience along the way. Do not wait until after the 29 days are over to reflect. You could very well miss opportunities if you wait.

Remember that writing a list of the gifts that you consciously gave over the last month is not a reflection. Reflection goes much deeper than a description of the activities in which you participated.

Below are some additional questions to help guide your reflection.

Did you feel anxious or stressed in your day-to-day living before doing this *Ch'i Essential*? If so, then notice what you experience after a month of conscious giving. Your challenges are far fewer than Cami's. What did this experience do to your levels of stress and worry?

Did you notice any changes emotionally or any improvement to your self-esteem? Do you continue giving gifts after 29 days? Did you create a habit that honors you and the people around you?

---

a   Erich Fromm is a Social Psychologist and the author of *The Art Of Loving*

When do you know that you are asleep? When you wake up. It is the same with consciousness. You only know that you were unconscious after you become conscious. Are you more conscious and present in your daily activities as a result of this *Ch'i Essential* activity?

How long did it take you to give a gift each day? How long does it take to hold a door open for someone? How long does it take to smile at someone? A second or two? Isn't it interesting that it only takes a couple of seconds to create a habit that lifts your energy, puts positive energy out into the world, and increases your consciousness.

Inspiration[1]

THE STORY OF LISA'S ROSES

"Do something nice for someone today" sounds like a platitude, but in Coatesville, PA, just a few miles away from West Chester University's campus, this is a wonderful legacy and memorial to the outpouring of love from the community and friends of Lisa DePedro. This is another true story, much like Cami Walker's, where people put energy out into the world while connecting with each other to create healing power.

Greg and Dorrie DePedro, owners of the Coatesville Flower Shop, honor the memory of their daughter Lisa in a unique way. Lisa was a young mother who died of cancer at the age of 30 in 2004. As she was dying, Lisa received more offers of help than she knew what to do with. Overwhelmed, she told people that instead of helping her, they should do something nice for someone else. Due to this brave woman's opening of her heart to lift others during her challenging time, Lisa's Roses was born.

Each year on August 23rd, magic happens that moves loving energy out into the world, honoring Lisa's legacy of "Do something nice for someone today." Anyone who walks into the Coatesville Flower Shop on this special day and asks is given a dozen roses. But there is one caveat. You can keep one rose for yourself, but you must give the remainder of the roses away to eleven different people, doing something nice for them.

My wife, daughters, and granddaughters participate in this beautiful consciousness raising day, sharing the gifts of Lisa's Roses by visiting with the DePedro's and then taking their beautiful flowers to the local super-

"I expect to pass through this world but once; any good thing that I can do, or any kindness that I can show to any fellow creature, let me do it now. Let me not defer or neglect it for I shall not pass this way again."

STEPHAN GIRARD

market to give them away. They get to enjoy the smiles created by this wonderful spread of kindness out into the world.

Not only are the DePedros spreading kindness, but they have become mentors to mothers and fathers who have lost children. It's not something they had planned to do; it's something they do to honor their daughter.

August 23rd is now observed nationally with the spread of kindness and consciousness. The first year, the Coatesville Flower Shop gave out about 5,000 dozen roses. In the last few years they gave out about 10,000 dozen of "Lisa's Smiles." Figures from 2009 stated that close to 800 more flower shops participated in giving out roses in other cities across Pennsylvania, New York, California, Florida, Virginia, Texas, North Carolina and Wisconsin.[2] Can you imagine what those figures have blossomed to today?

SPECIAL INVITATION

Living in this wonderful global village with the Internet connecting all of us, Cami Walker reached out to me via email, writing: "I am honored that you use 29 Gifts in such a dedicated way. Thank you for you dedication and support." We should all send a "Thank You" note to Ms. Walker who has lifted the bar on mindfulness and connection for all of us and whose generosity of Spirit is truly incredible.

What's more, Cami has graciously extended a Special Invitation to the readers of *Tai Chi and the Art of Mindfulness* to share their experiences with the 29 Gifts *Ch'i Essential*. You can officially sign up to become a part of the 29 Gifts community at www.29Gifts.org. Here you can post your stories and reflections about what participating in the 29 Gifts activity has meant to you and how it has affected your journey. You are also invited to be a part of her Facebook community. You can find it at www.facebook.com/29gifts. I suggest that you "Like" the page and help support the mindfulness that Cami shares throughout the world.

11

Non-Shoulder Form

THINK ABOUT YOUR SHOULDERS. How do they feel right now? Relaxed? Raise them up toward your ears, then drop them, only do it really slow. How do they feel now?

Most people hold tension in their shoulders and are not even aware that they are doing it. Do you ever crunch your shoulders up when you are deep in thought, thinking hard and trying to solve a problem? Adding stress and tension to your body will not help you think better.

For the next week, you get to practice an entire Tai Chi-style form called the Non-Shoulder Form. In Tai Chi, there are no shoulders. They are not used in any of the movements or exercises. The shoulders should always hang relaxed and comfortable. This is their natural position. Think of your shoulders as a clothes hanger and your body as a suit of clothes, hanging, suspended and relaxed, calm and comfortable.

To practice the Non-Shoulder Form, let your head float up as if suspended from above by a string. This is the Tai Chi Principle of Upright or vertical spine. Allow your chin to relax in a downward position. This position protects your throat. Let go of your shoulders, and most important, think *"Relax,"* while taking a breath deep into your *Dan Tien* (your abdomen). Notice what happens when your mindful awareness grows as you release tension and stress from your body.

Do this several times a day, when you are standing, walking, or even sitting. Notice what you experience as you continue to do the Non-Shoulder Form for a week. You are beginning to create a habit that honors you and your physiology. Plus, you are also applying the Principle of Letting Go as you release all tension in your shoulders, neck and upper back. The Tai Chi posture you are practicing will also help you look elegant. Photographers know about this kind of alignment, and their work reflects this knowledge of elegant posing. You can often see the same alignment with actors, movie stars, and models. Who knows, maybe you can make it onto the cover of *Rolling Stone*. Wouldn't that be nice for your Reflection Journal entry?

An Amazing Life
Modify Your Rules & Criteria

PART B

REREAD YOUR RULES AND CRITERIA, your detailed description of what an amazing life looks like for you.

Now consider the possibility of having fewer rules. Or consider relaxing your criteria of what needs to happen or what you need to accomplish before you can say you are living an amazing life. What would this shift do to your outlook? How would you feel? Could you be living an amazing life much sooner than you previously believed possible?

Continue to examine your rules and criteria. Are there any in your list that do not honor you? Are there "must dos" and "must haves" that will take a long time to accomplish? Consider dropping some of these items from your list.

How about dropping the entire list altogether and having no rules? This is a bold move. Consider that maybe you can be living an amazing life right now! You don't have to wait to accomplish anything. Can you be living an amazing life while you are attempting to accomplish everything that you would like to do?

Living an "Amazing Life" could be just like Tai Chi. Tai Chi is how you do what you do. It is how you focus and what you focus on. Maybe your life can be amazing as you work to graduate from college. Or maybe it

can be amazing as you move towards obtaining that fabulous job with its six-figure income. Or maybe life can be amazing even before you meet your perfect mate.

Tai Chi is an internal art, one that uses the heart-mind. With our mind and with our thoughts, we set the *ch'i* in motion. We move energy to help us get to our dreams and desires in life. Write a reflection in which you consider having fewer rules or having no rules at all in order to be able to say that you are living an amazing life.

"I am still determined to be cheerful and happy in whatever situation I may be, for I have also learned from experience that the greater part of our happiness or misery depends upon our dispositions and not upon our circumstances."

MARTHA WASHINGTON

"The happiness of your life depends upon the quality of your thoughts, therefore guard accordingly; and take care that you entertain no notions unsuitable to virtue, and reasonable nature."

MARCUS AURELIUS ANTONINUS

13

Five Wants and Five Don't Wants

PART A

WHAT DO YOU WANT IN LIFE? If you are going to focus on your dreams and desires, you need to define them. This *Ch'i Essential* will help you become clear on what you want most from life.

Many times people do not know what they want. If you do not know what you want, how will you recognize it when it shows up? You might actually miss the opportunity to get something you most desire just by being unaware or unconscious. If you are going to focus effectively on your dreams and desires, you need to be crystal clear on what they are.

What happens when you walk into a restaurant and the waitperson comes to your table and asks, "What you would like to order?" If you do not know, do they bring you food? Of course not. Maybe it works the same way in the buffet we call life.

Often, if you are not clear on what you want, it is sometimes easier to approach things in reverse. Sometimes you know right away what you do not want. You might not want to be late to class or work. You might not want to get sick. Or get in a car accident. Or breakup with your girlfriend or boyfriend.

For Part A of this *Ch'i Essential* activity, you will make up two short five-item lists.

1.   List the top five things you want in your life.

2.   List the top five things that you do not desire in your life.

Be specific in your lists. Be really clear on what you want and what you do not want. Envision these things in vivid detail and put them in your lists.

Clarifying

Five Wants and

Five Don't Wants

PART B

MOST OF OUR DAILY THOUGHTS that originate in the Monkey Mind come from our "Don't Wants." This is negative energy. For example:

> I don't want to be late to class.

> I don't want to break up with my girlfriend/boyfriend.

> I don't want to get into an accident.

Next there are the "If Only" thoughts. They are in the same category, but they are a bit more of the stealth Monkey Mind variety of thoughts. They are basically "Don't Want" thoughts about the past. For example:

> If only I had gotten that job.

> If only she would have gone out with me.

> If only I had 'aced' that exam.

All of these thoughts are both conscious and unconscious. Quantum Physics suggests that any thought tied to strong emotions, either positive or negative, will attract events of similar energy into our lives.

For example, ever notice how, when things seem to be going wrong, it is often a string of several events in and around the same time frame. You are running late for class. Then you cannot find your car keys. Next, you get to campus and can't find a parking space near your classroom. You finally find a space, and then you accidentally tap the fender of the car in front of you, causing a minor dent. Notice how all these events contain a similar negative energy.

But the good news is that this clustering also works the same way with positive energy. Imagine that it is Thursday and you finally see the person whom you have been attracted to in the library. You muster up the nerve to ask the person out, and immediately the person says "yes," and then tells you that he or she has been thinking about you too. That afternoon, you go to your biology class and the exam results are distributed, the one you thought you did terribly on. It turns out that you earned an "A." Later that afternoon, you are psyched thinking about your date the next night, but then you remember that you do not get paid until next week. You go back to your apartment only to find a card from your Uncle Phil who forgot your birthday last month. Inside the card is a check for $100. You are suddenly flush and all set for your date. Again, notice how all of these events contain a similar energy. This time it's positive energy.

Are both of these scenarios coincidences, or is something else going on? If you find yourself in either type of situation, I invite you to examine your emotions and thoughts surrounding these events. How do they feel to you? This reflection could give you insight into what your vibrational energy is.

Quantum Physics again suggests that any thought you hold onto for sixteen seconds or more, while at the same time tying that thought to strong emotions, either positive or negative, will result in the manifestation of things or events in your life with a similar vibration.

With this *Ch'i Essential* activity, you will test these energetic ideas. In addition, if these theories are correct, you will be inviting your dreams and desires into your life.

Rewrite your "Five Wants" in present tense. Write out your "wants" as if they are already in your life. Feel them here, now. Own them. Use empowering language, words that motivate you, words that get you excited about life. Add specific details. For example, if you want that beach house, where is it? What color is it? How many rooms does it have? What are the views like? Did you include the swimming pool? And don't forget the waterslide.

Or, if one of the items on your "want" list is that you want to be rich, then be more specific. How rich? Rich in family and friends, or Bill Gates rich? And what will you do with that money? Do you want to be rich enough to cure cancer? In fact, there is a multi-billionaire living in South Africa who is working on doing just that.

Next take your "Don't Wants" and reverse them, making them positive. For example: "I don't want to be sick," now becomes, "I'm enjoying vibrant health now. I'm grateful for my strong mind and body, and that I can actively participate in any activity of my choosing."

Or you can rewrite "I don't want to be bankrupt and poor," as "I have a full and overflowing bank account," or, "Money comes to me easily and frequently." Again, using empowering language is a key to testing these ideas and principles.

You have now created a ten-item list of what you want most in life. Read your list twice a day. Read it each morning before you get out of bed, and again each night before you go to sleep. It will only take about a minute or less. Fill yourself with positive feelings and emotions as you begin to focus on your dreams and desires. Feel them as if they are a part of your life now. Get your brain excited about the possibilities. Do this for two weeks and then write a reflection. Consider the possibility that reading your list is changing your day-to-day.

Tai Chi teaches that how we focus our attention and intention can be a game changer. This is what sets the *ch'i* in motion, the energy to fuel your dreams and your journey.

TRANQUILTY

Five Things You Really, Really Like About Yourself

PART A

MAKE A LIST OF FIVE QUALITIES that you really, really like about yourself. Are you smart? Do you have a good sense of humor? Maybe you are loyal to friends and family. Do you have integrity? Are you honest? Compassionate? Caring? Loving?

When writing your list of the five things you really, really like about yourself, use empowering language. Remember, words hold energy. How empowering can you make your list? How much *ch'i* can you fill your descriptions with?

智

WISDOM

16

Three Ways to Practice Tai Chi All Day Long

THERE ARE THREE MOVEMENTS THAT we do over and over again in Tai Chi.

1. Stepping the foot

2. Shifting the weight

3. Turning the waist

When you separate stepping the foot from shifting weight onto it, you get to experience Yin–Yang in the Principle of Empty and Full. When you turn the waist, you allow the *Dan Tien*, your Sea of *Ch'i*, to lead the movement.

This is a wonderful way to relax and grow your mindful awareness whenever you are standing. For example, you get that all-important phone call, the one that has the potential to create tension. Maybe it is a job interview, or setting up an internship. This is the perfect time to stand up and think *relax*. Step one foot and rest it on the ground empty. Next, sink into the ground as you pour weight from one foot to the other. Feel your weight melt into the floor as you relax and prepare your mind to function better. Lift the toes and pivot on your heel, turning your waist.

Or lift your heel and pivot on the toes. Then step the other foot and start all over again. Notice the clarity of mind begin to emerge.

This is a fun *Ch'i Essential* to do in the grocery store checkout line during lunchtime. People are generally uptight, waiting to pay for their items and hurry back to work or class. Out of nowhere appears this little old man or little old lady at the front of the line, painfully counting out their change. Next comes the rummaging through his or her pockets, trying to find their coupons and perhaps a frequent shopper card. You look around and see that the rest of the people in line are having meltdowns, getting aggravated, or worse. You witness all the negative energy crossing their faces and in their body postures. Meanwhile, you get to practice Tai Chi in stealth mode. Simply think *relax*. Let your head float up and start melting into the ground, into one foot and then the other. You'll be the only person in line with a big smile across your face, relaxing and enjoying the scene.

Do this *Ch'i Essential* activity for one week and notice how much of a difference it can make.

"I am always doing that which I cannot do, in order that I may learn how to do it."

PABLO PICASSO

Do Something You Think You Can't

"Everyday do something you think you can't."

CHIN-NING CHU[a]

DO YOU INSULATE YOURSELF FROM new experiences? Are you hesitant to try to eat something that you are not sure you will like? Do you avoid engaging a person with whom you disagree? Then rest assured, those chicken fingers and fries will always be there at your favorite fast food joint.[1] You can count on that.

People often create unconscious habits that not only limit the possibilities in their thinking but also inhibit growth opportunities. These are the rules we follow without thinking about them. They are rules that help us play it safe. They are known entities for us. These rules have become unconscious habits because they have always worked before.

What if "new" became your conscious habit? How empowering would it be to actually do something you thought you could not?

Monotony is a Flow killer. It's doing the same thing, over and over again, day after day. Do you always drive the same route to school or work?

"Be open to the impossibilities."

MEYER D. GOLDFARB
MY DAD & SUPERHERO

a   Chin-ning Chu was a motivational speaker and bestselling author. Ms. Chu wrote books empowering women in business through the application of Taoist ideas and philosophy.

Sometimes we repeat something so many times that it becomes a habit. Unfortunately, it becomes an unconscious habit that makes us stiff and stuck in our ways without even knowing it. It also takes us out of Flow.[2]

A PRACTICAL APPLICATION OF YOUR FOCUS

There is positive stimulation to grow the brain and negative stimulation to grow the brain. You wire new neuronal connections and shape your brain with your focus, whether you are conscious about it or not.[3] Doing something you think you cannot do or learning new movements in Tai Chi create positive connections.

"Twenty years from now you'll be more disappointed by the things you didn't do than by the things you did do."

MARK TWAIN

IDEAS & SUGGESTIONS

1. Brush your teeth with your left hand if you are right-handed or vice versa. I do this with my first brushing everyday. It wasn't pretty at first because I use an electric toothbrush. If fact, it was a little scary in the beginning, but now I can do it. It starts my day off with a conscious reminder to "do something I think I can't."

2. Tie your sneaker laces backwards. Have the rabbit run around the tree in the other direction. In other words, loop the lace around the other way. There is actually science behind this type of tie supporting a stronger knot. You will get fewer flat tires (untied shoelaces). Most mothers know about this approach.

3. If you do not think that you are an artist, then this idea is perfect for you. Try drawing by copying a picture, only turn the picture upside down before you start. Your brain will not be able to muck up the perspective.[4]

For this *Ch'i Essential* activity, look for something that you can con-sciously do differently today. This exercise keeps you flexible and brings you into conscious Flow.

WORDS OF CAUTION

Do not try to fly off of the rooftop of Anderson Hall. And, do not try and stop a truck by walking into the street. Practice safety first. I want you around to finish this workbook.

One final word of caution, from the brilliant insight of legendary actor and comedian Dick Van Dyke:[5]

> *"You can spread jelly on the peanut butter,*
> *but don't try to spread peanut butter on the jelly."*

"Whoever is stiff and inflexible is a disciple of death. Whoever is soft and yielding is a disciple of life. The hard and stiff will be broken. The soft and supple will prevail."

LAO-TZU

TAO TE CHING

天使

ANGEL

Mind Power
Focus on Something

THIS IS A *CH'I ESSENTIAL* to test the power of your mind and to explore the power of your ability to focus without effort. "Without effort" points to doing your day-to-day Tai Chi style.

For the next week, focus on something and see if you can find more of your object of focus. What does this mean? For example, do you own a car? If so, can you remember the first day that you got your car? It does not matter if the car is new or used, just try to remember the thrill you had driving it around on that first day. Can you remember what you noticed? Did you begin to see more of the same make and model vehicle that you own? All of a sudden, did it seem like everyone was driving a similar car everywhere you went?

Remember, what we think about and intend does in fact occur. This is quantum physics. This concept is especially powerful when co-partnered with Spirit.

This *Ch'i Essential* activity informs us that practices of mental training, which include Tai Chi and meditation, can be extremely beneficial to our journey through life.

FOCUS ON SOMETHING
REFLECTION JOURNAL TIPS

In addition to your reflection, consider the following questions:

1. What does it mean that you see more of what
    you focus on?

2. How can you use this information to your
    advantage?

3. Considering the amount of effort it took you to
    focus on something, what did you learn about
    the power of your mind?

The Switch

Five Things You Really, Really Like About Yourself

REDUX

THE SWITCH IS A *CH'I ESSENTIAL* that focuses on creating a habit of "thoughts that honor you." Take out your list of the "Five Things You Really, Really Like About Yourself" (see *Ch'i Essential* 15). Now rewrite them, filling their description with positive emotion, energy and words that empower you.

For example, let's say that one of the things you wrote is "I'm a good problem solver." Then rewrite it something like this: "I have brilliant insight, always seeing solutions where other people only see problems. There is a way and I will definitely find it."

USING THE SWITCH TO CREATE THOUGHTS THAT HONOR YOU

You now have five empowering things that you really, really like about yourself. Each one of them is a magical "switch," one that you will flip on, just like flipping on a light switch when you enter a dark room. You can use one each day, or rotate through your all of your magical switches, using several of them throughout the course of your day.

You are now going to employ this new technology to release the Monkey Mind and still the negative thoughts that it brings along. In fact, the way to explore the power of this *Ch'i Essential* is to make a little game of it.

For the next week, whenever the Monkeys rear their ugly heads with a negative thought, like, "I don't have enough time," or "I'm going to be late for work again," use your special switch. Simply tell yourself, "But I have brilliant insight, always seeing solutions where other people only see problems. There is always a way and I will definitely find it."

Notice how you feel when you flip your "switch" and change the direction of your mind and the thoughts that you are focusing on. You are beginning to clean up your thinking and focus on what empowers you.

An alternative approach would be to use humor and create a "switch" like, "I have really good hair." For example, the next time your Monkey Mind

THE SWITCH
REFLECTION JOURNAL TIPS

In addition to the questions listed in the "Reflection and Insight Journal" section, feel free to include what you have experienced when using your magical "switch" to interrupt the Monkey Mind. Please consider the following:

1.   How do you want to be in the world?

2.   What kind of thoughts do you want to cultivate as you journey through life?

What happens within creates and informs your experiences on the outside. And you get to choose what happens when you are conscious.

is telling you, "You'll never find a parking spot," just think, "But I have really good hair." You just might crack yourself up, moving from negative energy and tension to a lighter, brighter thought.

Have fun with your magical switches. Feel free to change them up. Rather than resisting your Monkey Mind thoughts or making yourself wrong once you realize what these negative thoughts are doing to you, you get to practice the Tai Chi Principle of Non-Resistance. Simply changing what you focus on and how you focus does create habits and thoughts that honor and empower you.

The Monkey Mind thoughts are basically unconscious habits. It is your "self-talk" that takes you out of Flow. When the little voice in your head says: "I'll never get a date with so-and-so," or "I can't sing," or "I'm not an 'A' student," flip your special "switch." These thoughts are like the movie *Groundhog's Day*. There is never anything new from the Monkey Mind. It is that old negative self-talk over and over and over again, day after day.

The "Switch" creates an opportunity for you to also practice the "Principle of Letting Go." Part of the practice of "Letting Go" is not worrying about the idea of letting go. In fact, don't worry about letting go at all. Just be okay with "what is."

With its focus on the negative thoughts, the Monkey Mind, is a negative motivation. Instead, in Tai Chi, we create new habits, ones that honor us and help us along our journey, by replacing bad habits with new empowering ones.

Inspiration[1]

"If you are distressed by anything external, the pain is not due to the thing itself, but to your estimate of it; and this you have the power to revoke at any moment."

MARCUS AURELIUS
ANTONINUS

FIRE

Road Rage

THIS *CH'I ESSENTIAL* IS A PRACTICAL activity to use your mind to change your energy, and even make you feel better. The use of *Xin Yi*, the heart-mind, is imperative in Tai Chi. It is intention, the intention to relax and nurture. Without the mind, it is not Tai Chi.

Did a vehicle ever cut you off when you are driving down the highway? Or maybe someone in front of you changed lanes abruptly without looking, causing you to slam on the brakes?

Or perhaps you were cruising along, and then got stuck behind someone who is hunkered down in the left lane, going 20 miles-per-hour under the speed limit, and would not let you pass?

How about this? Maybe you are running late for a meeting and get stuck behind someone who is driving far too slow and swerving. You grit your teeth and impatiently wait the long 15 minutes before you can safely pass him on the right only to see that he is texting and lost in his smart phone.

How do you feel when one of these circumstances happens to you? Do you get mildly agitated, or upset, or worse? And what happened to your energy and Flow?

When we are driving around in our car, there are numerous situations that get our blood boiling. What are the feelings that pass through your body when that happens? What is the energy of the emotions and thoughts you experience? Tension? Stress? Anger?

"For every minute you remain angry you give up sixty seconds of peace of mind."

RALPH WALDO EMERSON

And how long do you keep these negative feelings alive, constantly passing through your heart-mind over and over again? Until you can pass that little old son-of-a-gun who owns the left lane?

Are you one of those people who grips the steering wheel a little harder than usual, white-knuckling your way down the road? Or maybe you are the type of person who enjoys spittling the windshield as you hurl expletives, streaming from your mouth in ascending volume? In fact, most people never really learn to curse until they learn to drive.

We all know the feeling of road rage, that feeling of our pulse pounding in our ears, our breath shallow and choked. Most of us even know that it is not good for the old ticker. Yet there we are with this enormous burst of negative energy, invading our day.

Road rage is an activity of the mind. It is that old "somebody done somebody wrong" song. You are singing it, yelling and cursing at the top of your lungs, meanwhile, the person who cut you off does not even get to hear your performance. That person is already a half-mile down the road ahead of you.

So who is really being affected with all that negative energy? You? Your passengers? Did you really get even and teach that son-of-a-gun that interrupted your Flow a lesson?

For this *Ch'i Essential*, you will use you mind to change your energy, and maybe, if you are lucky, even brighten your day a little.

The next time a driver invades your calm on the highway, instead of giving him the middle finger salute, send that person prayers and blessings. Surround him with love and light.

You laugh? What is this, some New Age mumbo jumbo? Light and love? Are you kidding me?

Do you think it is impossible to bless someone who has just cut you off with his unconscious behavior? Just like road rage is an activity of the mind, so is sending prayers and blessings.

Here is a suggestion to use your heart-mind to change your energy. Tell yourself a little story. Imagine that the person who just cut you off is a young mother racing to the hospital with an injured child. What you cannot see, and what you do not know, is that her child fell out of a tree and is lying bloody on the back seat of the car. It is now a matter of life or death that this mother gets her child to the hospital as soon as possible. Notice how this changes your energy and what you feel in your body. It is not difficult to send prayers and blessings now. Plus, you get to practice the Tai Chi Principle of Slowing Down.

Do this *Ch'i Essential* for one week. Are you creating a habit that honors you? Maybe you are replacing a habit that got your blood boiling at the same time. Now you can enjoy the scenery.

SINCERITY

21

Get Curious

DO YOU FEEL THAT YOU are present all of the time? How about being present most of the time? Or, at least, some of the time?

What is the big deal about the present moment—the "Now?" Why all the to-do about being fully present in the moment? The present only lasts a few minutes and then it is gone.[1]

Think about the pros and cons of being present and decide for yourself.

Ever feel like you are waiting? Waiting for a bus? Or waiting for the phone to ring? Or how about waiting for a friend to show up? Whenever you are waiting, you are practicing some form of inner resistance or negative energy. It means that you do not like the present moment. When you do not like the present, your focus is on what is wrong with the moment.

Tai Chi teaches you to let go of resistance, physically, emotionally, and psychologically. Instead of practicing inner resistance, you learn to practice "being."[2]

Being present can be fun. Ever get lost in the moment? We often do when we are having fun and enjoying ourselves. It's "effortless effort," a desired state in your Tai Chi practice.

How do you become present? The study of Tai Chi, meditation, and yoga all share the secrets as to how to practice "being," and being present. Any activity that connects the mind and body generates presence. Your body is an anchor to the present moment.

"The trick is to say yes to life."

JAMES BALDWIN

AMERICAN NOVELIST, ESSAYIST, PLAYWRIGHT, POET, AND SOCIAL CRITIC

In addition, most of us are present when we are having fun, hanging with our friends and family. Any engaging activity creates presence. Consider painting, or playing an instrument, or singing, or sports. If you have ever experienced downhill skiing, then you know about being present.

Have you ever traveled alone for a long period of time and felt trapped on a plane, train, or bus? Were you bored? Being bored is another stealth version of the Monkey Mind. It is resisting the present moment. When you are feeling bored, your mind is focused on the future, on another moment in time when you think that you will feel different, when you think that your life will be exciting again.

Another way to generate presence is to become curious. When traveling alone, start a conversation with a stranger. Be curious. Ask questions. Listen. Be there. Pay attention and things change. You could actually en-

CURIOSITY BUSINESS TOOLS

Becoming curious is also a wonderful business tool. Questions sparked by curiosity can promote growth and insight in any arena. Asking "why" is a great way to start.[3] Consider the following:

1. Why do things work this way?

2. Why is that your goal?

And if you really want to discover important information, ask:

3. Why did you say no?

4. Why are we treating people differently?

5. Why did you change your mind?

6. My favorite curiosity question is: "Why not?"

joy yourself and make a new friend. An unpublished writer friend did this on a plane to the west coast. As it turned out, the person he was sitting with was a screenwriter. One thing led to another, and with a little help, my friend got that long awaited book deal. Guess what he put in his Evidence Journal?

You can also become curious by looking at a person's face. See all the amazing colors there. People are not just one color. There are hundreds and thousands of shades of colors and textures on a person's face. Plus, there is hair—eyebrows, beards, mustaches, etc.—not to mention makeup and clothes. Notice as much as you can about a person while observing or conversing with him or her.

When you go outside, especially in Spring or Summer, notice all the millions of shades of green. These are colors that we see nearly every day, yet we often fail to notice them. We think, "Oh, it's a tree," or "That's grass," and then dismiss from our consciousness what we are looking at. We have stopped really seeing. We have left the present. Becoming curious brings you into the "Now," the present moment. There is a malady called Nature Deficit Disorder. It refers to a wide range of behavioral problems as a result of spending less time outdoors.[4] In addition, the explosion in the use of technology contributes to negative connections in our brains and Nature Deficit Disorder.[5] Being curious in nature can help prevent or counteract this.

Be curious once a day for the next week. Consciously consider what you notice. See how much presence you can generate and notice how that feels. Consider what this *Ch'i Essential* did to your attention span after one week. Maybe you have reversed some of the effects of technology on your brain when you are living deep in your smart phone, or lost on your tablet or computer. What is different in your day-to-day when you are focused on getting curious?

I wonder why. I wonder why.
I wonder why I wonder.
I wonder why I wonder why
I wonder why I wonder!

RICHARD P. FEYNMAN

DESTINY

Intention

WHAT ARE YOU THINKING? Would you like this thought to create your life? Thoughts do create your life, and once you can understand that, you can make enormous changes.[1]

Remember, quantum physics informs us that what we think about and intend does occur. This phenomenon is especially powerful when copartnered with Spirit. This combination is the power of the mind.

Tai Chi teaches you to use the heart-mind, *Xin Yi*, which is best understood in our western culture as an intention. In Tai Chi you start with the intention to relax; that is, the intention to nurture and honor your physiology and yourself. The mind, using an intention, sets the *ch'i* or universal energy in motion. We then explore and learn to do what Grandmaster Benjamin Lo instructs: "Use *ch'i* and not muscle." The mind, as well as intention, is the Tai Chi part of the movements.

Ch'i is everywhere in your life and is not limited to your Tai Chi practice. For the next two weeks, you will do an experiment and start each day with an intention. Set your intention the night before for the next day. Think about it as soon as you wake up and see what manifests.

When setting your intention, do it with feeling. Feelings and emotions contain energy. How much energy can you move? In addition, if thoughts do create your life, how did you word your vision for the next day? Was it empowering? Inspiring? Motivating?

We have up to 100,000 thoughts each day. When you are awake sixteen hours every day, you are experiencing almost two thoughts every second. What can you do with a couple of thoughts? Tai Chi trains you to recognize the power of your internal resources, and to tap into the power of your mind.

SETTING AN INTENTION: WEEK 1

Setting an intention is playing with energy, *ch'i*. Here are a few suggestions to get you started:

1. Set an intention to find a parking spot.

2. Set an intention to do well in an upcoming meeting.

3. Set an intention to get all your work done and still have energy to go out and socialize with your friends.

"The starting point of all achievement is desire. Keep this constantly in mind. Weak desires bring weak results, just as a small fire makes a small amount of heat."

NAPOLEON HILL

*"It is not enough to have a good mind;
the main thing is to use it well."*

RENÉ DESCARTES

SETTING AN INTENTION: WEEK 2

For the second week, consciously expand your intentions beyond your "to do" list. Discover how much energy you can create and move. Explore the power of your thoughts. For example:

1. If you will be taking a long car ride, set an intention to reach your destination safely, feeling refreshed, recharged and energized.

2. Set an intention to enjoy your day or your week.

3. Set an intention to flow effortlessly through your day, enjoying all the activities and people that cross your path.

4. Set an intention to get a good night's sleep, to wake up energized and recharged, and feeling great.

5. Set an intention to attract blessings into your life. Also, set the intention to allow your blessings to reveal themselves. How would your day change if you noticed all your blessings in real time, while they were happening?

FRIENDSHIP

23

"When I was 5 years old, my mother always told me that happiness was the key to life. When I went to school, they asked me what I wanted to be when I grew up. I wrote down 'happy.' They told me I didn't understand the assignment, and I told them they didn't understand life."

JOHN LENNON

Happiness Criteria

DO YOU WANT TO BE HAPPY? Of course you do. Everyone wants to feel happy. This *Ch'i Essential* activity is an excellent opportunity to take a good look at what makes you happy and what contributes to your joy in life.

Happiness is often very different for different people. Maybe happiness is a good meal, or hanging with your friends and family, or playing with your dog, or sitting on a beach and watching a sunset with your significant other.

For your Reflection Journal, use the follow questions to help guide your thoughts on defining your happiness criteria.

1. What makes you happy?
    What will make you feel like you are happy?

2. What goes into happiness for you?

3. When you feel happy, what is going on?
    Are you engaged in an activity?
    Or is it the person or people that you are with?
    Or is it just a mindset?

4. What contributes to your happiness?

5. If happiness is not a state of its own, then what does it appear to be a by-product of?

6. Finish the following sentences:
    I can be happy if . . .
    I'll be happy when . . .

"The Constitution only guarantees the American people the right to pursue happiness. You have to catch it yourself."

BEN FRANKLIN

BELIEVE

Manifest Magic
In One Year

QUANTUM PHYSICS, STEM-CELL BIOLOGISTS, and Nobel Prize winning chemists all agree that thoughts create your life and even affect your biology, including changes in your brain in ways that can be measured and observed in scans and fMRIs.[1] With that in mind, take some relaxed meditative time to think. Reflect on your desires and goals, and open your heart to all the possibilities. Contemplate on what you intend to manifest for yourself, for your loved ones, and for your community in the next year.

Feel yourself accomplishing your dreams now, in present time. Remember, in Tai Chi practice, as well as in life, *it is not what you do, but how you do it*. Focus on the mindfulness with which you fill your life with as you move toward what you intend to manifest. How does that feel?

To show how powerful this thinking about intention can be, consider firewalkers. Firewalkers are people who walk barefoot over red-hot coals, which are placed in beds twelve-feet long or longer, with temperatures ranging from 1,200 to 1,500 degrees Fahrenheit – hot enough to cause third-degree burns. If people can walk on fire and not get burned using their thoughts and their respective states of consciousness, what can you manifest in one year? Use your consciousness and mindful awareness to

create the life you desire. By the way, I have participated in a firewalk, and didn't even roast my little piggies. It was quite an empowering experience.[a]

This activity will help you begin to harness the power of intentions. Your Reflection Journal entry should be more than a "to do" list or a shopping list of items that you merely check off when completed. Consider how you are moving energy and pushing out your *ch'i*. How are you connecting with the people around you? What does your contribution look like to yourself, to your friends and family, as well as to your community?

a Please do not try firewalking on your own. Seek out a trained professional to assist you.

WHAT WILL YOU MANIFEST IN A YEAR? REFLECTION JOURNAL TIPS

Write down your desires and intentions of what you intend to manifest during the next year. Allow yourself to step into your dreams and desires of what and how you want your life to be.

Remember, thoughts do create your life. You hold the power to make enormous changes.

1. How did your journal entry make you feel?

2. How did you describe your vision? Was it empowering? Inspiring? Motivating?

3. What's the most daring version of your vision? Test the power and creativity of your mind with this *Ch'i Essential*.

Just for fun, mark your calendar for one year from now. When the date rolls around, reread your essay and compare it to your current reality. How did you do? I invite you to send me an email with your discoveries.   mitch@mitchgoldfarb.com

25

"All children are born artists."

PABLO PICASSO

Invent One Thing

ARE YOU AFRAID OF BEING WRONG? Or have you ever been afraid of making a mistake? Fear is a stealth version of the Monkey Mind. When you feel fear, you are practicing inner resistance.

Kids are great teachers. They are willing to take a chance. If they do not know, they will have a go at it. They will try something new. They're not frightened of being wrong the way adults are. Many adults have lost the capacity to embrace new things, especially if they do not know how to do them. Remember, if you're not prepared to be wrong, you'll not come up with anything new, or original, or of value. You will play it safe and just do what someone else did before you.

We live in a culture that stigmatizes mistakes. This is merely a mindset, one that does not empower or honor anyone. In fact, it will steal your *ch'i*, your personal power.

Most people mistakenly think that we grow into creativity. But not Picasso. He tells us something different. Picasso's statement suggests that the challenge is to remain an artist as we grow up. People do not grow into creativity; they grow out of it. Often we are educated out of it and taught to play it safe.[1]

What if you were not afraid of failure? What if you knew that you would succeed, no matter what? Keeping that in mind, if you could invent one thing that could make your life and everyone else's life easier, what would it be?

Take the time to cultivate the richness of your human capacity. Cheng Man-Ching called Tai Chi the *"art of self-cultivation."* Use this as an opportunity to cultivate your creative capacities. Help bring new ideas into the world. Be part of the story of advancing human potential with the power of your mind and your thoughts. Keep your imagination alive. You might even surprise yourself.

26

Field Of Awareness

YOU ARE NOT A PERSON. You are a field of awareness, an alert presence.[1] This field or presence is your consciousness. The Field of Awareness *Ch'i Essential* will help you to use your consciousness and your mindful awareness to experience, explore, and interact with the world.

We often forget our connection to others, even the very people serving and waiting on us, as we get lost in our day-to-day minutia, consumed by all of our tasks and activities. This is a form of unconsciousness, subtle as it may be. This form of unconsciousness is a stealth condition of the Monkey Mind; thus, it is a disconnect from life.

Have you ever gone into a quick mart or convenience store, only to see the people in line at the checkout counter completely ignoring the person who is waiting on them or worse? Consider the scenario of the person who stops to pick up a pack of gum or buy a cup of coffee, and the cashier, the person who is actually making change and serving them, is being treated as an obstacle to that person returning to their car and getting on with their day. No eye contact is made. The customer could even be lost on his smart phone and just sticks his hand out without looking up when the cashier hands him change.

Or maybe you have witnessed a table of hungry people in a restaurant interacting with their server. Their waitperson, the person taking their order, often becomes a hostility target, an impediment, slowing down the food from being delivered to the table.

This is a *Ch'i Essential* where you practice *"being"* and connecting to your consciousness in the present moment. When you are conscious, you are an alert presence. Simply put, you are a "Field of Mindful Awareness."

Here is your *Ch'i Essential* activity. The next time you go into a store to make a purchase, give the person who waits on you your fullest attention. Rather than focusing on the products that you are purchasing, make the person who is serving you more important than the material things of the world. The human being who you are engaging with is now the primary purpose for the interaction. You are then practicing *"being."*

You do not need to speak or ask questions from the person serving you to give your fullest attention (but you can). Eye contact, or a smile, or body language, can be enough to let that person feel the gift of your presence. Make the human *being* more important than the things of the world. Use your "field of mindful awareness"—your consciousness—to experience, explore and interact with the world.

REFLECTION JOURNAL TIPS

1. What did you learn?

2. What was the point of this *Ch'i Essential* activity?

3. Notice how you feel after completing this activity.

4. Notice the energetic connection that you create with the people and the world around you.

In addition to the above suggestions, use the question list in the "Reflection and Insight Journal" section to deepen your inquiry and reflection.

27

Decluttering

PART A

DOES YOUR ENVIRONMENT STIMULATE or nurture you? Can you relax, unwind and recharge in it? Or maybe you want your environment to energize and rejuvenate you. Does it do that? Exactly what is your environment doing to you or for you?

This is a two-part *Ch'i Essential* where you will take a close look at your environment and all the stuff in it, and learn how it affects you.

Science tells us that all things are vibrating energy fields. In fact, nothing is really solid and motionless as it appears. When we look at a table or a chair on the molecular level, the atoms, electrons, and subatomic particles are moving. All physical matter is moving and vibrating energy.

In addition, many of the physical things in our environment, our stuff, can hold emotional energy. Maybe you have a seashell that you found walking on a beach with that special someone. Or maybe there is a photograph on your desktop that has captured an expression of joy on a loved one's face. How do these things make you feel when you see them?

Tai Chi teaches us how to cultivate our energy, *ch'i*, and use it in our daily lives. It is an internal art. We work from the inside out. But unlike some meditative arts, Tai Chi is practiced with the eyes open. We marry the mind, body, and Spirit, as well as the environment too. We want to understand what is happening energetically all around us. We want to be aware of it and recognize if it honors us or is otherwise an impediment, and then act accordingly.

All your stuff holds energy, and it affects you all the time, whether you are conscious of the energy you are bathing in or not. This Decluttering *Ch'i Essential* creates an opportunity for you to be consciously aware of what is around you and how it impacts you and your life energetically.

There is an ancient Buddhist practice of limiting your worldly possessions to 500 items. This includes your silverware, your socks and shoes, which both count as two items for every pair you own. You get the idea. In our modern day and age, this is a very difficult practice to embrace. For example, as a kid I owned a lot more than 500 baseball cards. And as an adult, I have much more than 500 songs in my smart phone.

Part of this ancient practice of limiting yourself to 500 items is to create freedom and freedom of movement. Imagine that you can pack up everything you own into a small suitcase and take off within 30 minutes. You are no longer tied down because of all your stuff.

In the movie *Fight Club*, Tyler Durden states: "The things you own, end up owning you." In our culture, we buy stuff to store our other stuff. Just go into any Home Depot or Lowes store around Christmas time and notice the huge variety of storage totes and containers on sale and prominently displayed in the aisles. We also insure our stuff, and we worry about our stuff. For example, if you own a car (and it does not matter if it is new or used), think back to that very first day you got your car. Did your Monkey Mind go crazy waiting for the very first scratch or ding to happen?

The good news is, do not despair and do not worry. With this Decluttering *Ch'i Essential*, you will not have to give away all of your possessions and go live on a mountaintop or deep in the woods somewhere. However, you will probably begin to realize that you do not need as much stuff as you think you do. In addition, getting rid of much of your stuff can be surprisingly liberating, as well as actually make you feel happier.

CLEARING FOR RECEIVING

The first part of this *Ch'i Essential* is clearing for receiving. You are going to take a look at your personal space and clear it out, thus neutralizing the energy in your environment. Everyone has a personal space that they can control. It could be your bedroom, or, if you have a roommate, than it can be your portion of the room, maybe the personal space around your bed. If you cannot use your room, then as a last resort, feel free to use the interior of your car if you have one. Some people are not even aware of all the stuff they have been collecting in their car. Is there a science experiment growing in that McDonald's bag that has been living on the floor in the back of your car for the last six months?

Take a look around at your personal space. Does the stuff you see honor you? Does it nurture you? How much stuff do you have around that you do not use? What are you focusing on unconsciously?

Visually, clutter can jumble your brain on an energetic level. Do you find that your attention is often distracted by the stuff in your environment when you sit down to study or get some work done?

DECLUTTER YOUR ENVIRONMENT

Take an inventory of all the stuff in your personal space. Next, make a list on a piece of paper using the following three categories and try to put each of your items into one of these categories.

1.   USEFUL:
     Is the item useful? For example, you use your desk for working or studying, or you use your lamp for reading.

2.   BEAUTIFUL:
     Does the item add beauty to your environment? Maybe it is a vase of flowers, or a nice picture on your wall.

3.   LOVING & SENTIMENTAL VALUE:
     Be careful with this category. You can easily put a lot of your stuff into this slot. Guard against being too sentimental and saving everything. Get clear on these items. Maybe you have a picture of your girlfriend or boyfriend, or your spouse, or your pet at home. You might also have a token from a special date or vacation that reminds you of a positive emotional experience.

NON-ESSENTIAL ITEMS

You now are left with several items that did not fall into any of the above three categories. These items are all non-essential. These are the items that you are to remove from your personal environment. Get rid of anything that is not useful, beautiful, or fails to fill you with a sense of joy. You have successfully identified all non-essential items, and now it is time to remove them and their energy from your space.

Do not worry. Just pack up all these non-essential items. Put them in a big Hefty trash bag or suitcase and place them in your basement, or the back of your closet, or the trunk of your car. When this *Ch'i Essential* is over, you have the option of bringing everything back into your room. You can even throw the dirty clothes back on the floor under your bed.

If you are really brave (although I do not advocate this action the first time you play with this *Ch'i Essential*), when you remove all your non-essential items, you can gift them forward. For example, you could offer them to a friend or take them to an organization, like Goodwill or the Salvation Army. You get the idea. This is what I did when I decluttered my closet. I let go of everything that I had not used in a year. I figured, if I really missed an item, I would go out and replace it with a new one. And guess what, I have never missed anything I gifted forward.

I also rewarded myself upon completion of decluttering my closet. I treated myself to one new item. Now, whenever I purchase something new, I remove something old and pass it forward, maintaining a balance.

FENG SHUI

This *Ch'i Essential* is the first part in a simplified version of Feng Shui. The ancient Chinese art of Feng Shui is based on the Taoist vision of understanding *ch'i* flow in nature and the environment. *Feng* means "wind" and *Shui* means "water." Wind and water are associated with goodhealth and fortune. The purpose is to stimulate positive *ch'i* flow in the environment and our lives, and to remove any blockages or obstacles preventing that flow.

In Tai Chi, you learn to build your personal *ch'i* and facilitate Flow in your life. Part A of this *Ch'i Essential* is clearing and neutralizing the energy in your environment. In Part B, you will get the opportunity to stimulate a specific energy to enhance your world. You will get to expand your *ch'i* and focus how it is used to support your journey in life.

Inspiration[1]

DECLUTTER YOUR ENVIRONMENT
REFLECTION JOURNAL TIPS

Complete the decluttering and clearing activity as soon as you can in order to have a week to experience the changes to your space and its new feel.

1. What energy shifts did you notice?

2. How do you feel when you enter your room?

3. How do you feel when you wake up in your changed environment?

4. What is the difference now as compared to how it felt before you cleared your room of non-essential items?

5. Does your room feel physically larger?

Remember, when doing the reflection in your journal, use the suggested questions in the "Reflection and Insight Journal" section for guidance. Writing down a list of items that you removed from your environment is not a contemplative act. Engage your inner nature, your heart-mind, as well as your mindful awareness.

You are now developing a new consciousness about your space and learning to be mindful of the energy around you.

GRATITUDE

Shawn Achor
The Happy Secret

USE THE LINK BELOW TO WATCH the short Shawn Achor TED Talk video "The Happy Secret to Better Work." (You can also search TED Talks, Shawn Achor, "The Happy Secret to Better Work.")

http://www.ted.com/talks/shawn_achor_the_happy_secret_to_better_work

Mr. Achor talks about positive psychology and happiness, which have roots in ancient philosophies. It is interesting when modern science begins to catch up to the ancient philosophies of Taoism, Confucianism, and Buddhism.

Do you notice that what Shawn Achor shares is the same as Tai Chi and its principles? What similarities can you find?

Where else do you notice Tai Chi in your daily life?

祝福

BLESS

Creating Sacred Space

DECLUTTERING: PART B

PART B OF THIS DECLUTTERING *Ch'i Essential* creates an opportunity for you to consciously act upon and stimulate your personal environment with a specific energy of your choosing. You get to express and promote the *ch'i* flow that you desire in your life, whether it is nurturing and soothing, or energizing and invigorating, or both.

Your living space, whether big or small, can be your sanctuary when you mindfully act upon it. In addition, these actions and choices help you to practice a mindful awareness during your day-to-day activities.

FENG SHUI

Feng Shui is a Taoist approach to space that involves looking at all the objects in a specific environment, from furniture to possessions, and then using principles of energy flow to design and plan the physical shape of a room and how it will be used.

When a new building is constructed, an architect is hired to design and oversee its construction. In Asian countries, a Feng Shui consultant resides among the same level of importance as an architect, and is hired to help with the design and oversight of a building. All of this is done to promote positive *ch'i* flow and remove any negative energy or block-

ages. Corporations and business enterprises have been using Feng Shui consultants for years to stimulate and create a favorable effect on the experience a customer has, the company's profits, and the growth of the business.

Think about the energy, your personal *ch'i*, that you would like to stimulate in your room. Is it a place where you will leave stress at the door and nurture your Spirit? Or would you like to boost your creativity and enhance your productivity, work, and career? Perhaps you would like to emphasize family and personal relationships, connections to the people you love and care about.

YOUR PERSONAL ALTAR

Once you have chosen the energy on which you wish to focus, you will create your own personal "sacred space" to stimulate that *ch'i* flow. One of the best ways to do this is by setting up a personal altar. To best enhance your mindfulness, I suggest placing your altar near your bed or in a special place just for you. A night table works great as it is the first thing you see in the morning upon waking up, and it is the last thing you see at night before going to sleep. You will then be able to bookend your day with positive energy and *ch'i* flow.

Place on your altar a few mindful symbols of your life, symbols that empower you, symbols that represent the energy you want to stimulate. Photographs hold energy. Choose a special photo, one just for you, and place it in a gold-colored frame. How do you feel when you see the smiling face of a loved one or significant other, or your family, or your pet dog or cat?

A single silk flower in a simple vase or a special candle can enhance beauty and calm. Try adding a seashell from a trip to the beach, one that reminds you of a person or the people with whom you shared a special time with. Or you could choose a small totem from a time when you felt Flow in your life, like a lift ticket when you went skiing.

Be mindful to create a positive mood and feeling for your sacred space, your personal altar, by selecting items and symbols that empower you and that exude the energy on which you would like to focus to enhance your daily journey.

Be careful not to clutter up your altar with too much stuff. Simplicity is key in setting up and focusing your energy.

Create your "sacred space" and setup your special altar as soon as you can. This way you will give yourself a week to experience the energy shift. Reflect on how you feel when you see each of your empowering symbols and totems daily. Is the change in energy just limited to your personal space or do you carry it with you out into the world as you go through your activities?

How does it feel being mindful of the energy in your environment?

LUCK

Five Questions

DO YOU EVER FEEL ANXIOUS? Do you experience anxiety when there is an upcoming test or exam? How about before that all-important business meeting or interview?

Here is a wonderfully insightful definition of anxiety.

> *"Anxiety is nothing but repeatedly re-experiencing failure in advance."*
>
> SETH GODIN

What a waste of time, effort, and energy it is to repeatedly re-experience failure in advance. Think about your upcoming exam. When you feel anxiety about the exam, you are focusing on failing the exam or at least getting many of the answers incorrect. The same holds true for closing that big deal or your upcoming sales presentation. If you are prepared, what is there to be anxious about?

In this *Ch'i Essential*, you get an opportunity to use the five questions[1] listed below to clear your Monkey Mind, release your anxiety, and create new thoughts that honor you.

FIVE QUESTIONS

Carry these five questions with you by writing them on a 3 x 5 card or popping them into your smart phone. Over the next week, whenever you have a thought that makes you feel anxious, pull out your question list and answer each one silently to yourself. It will take you less than a minute.

1.   Is it true?

2.   Can you absolutely know it's true?

3.   How do you react when you believe this thought?

4.   How would you be without the thought?

5.   Is it life threatening?

EXAMPLES

You start thinking that you will fail your upcoming biology exam. Now go through the questions.

1. Is it true that you are going to fail the biology exam? You tell yourself that you think so. That is what's creating the anxiety.

2. Can you absolutely know that it is true that you are going to fail the exam? Of course not. Nobody can see the future. If you can see the future, then go play the lottery and forget about the exam.

3. How do you react when you believe this thought? If you really believe that you are going to fail, then you experience anxiety. You get uptight. You are re-experiencing failing the exam in advance, over and over again.

4. How would you be without the thought? Would you be free? At peace? Back in Flow with your life?

5. Is it life threatening if you fail your exam? This is your reality check. Of course not. Life does go on after one biology exam.

"What you begin to notice as you strengthen (the brain) is the absence of the negative state."

DANIEL GOLEMAN, PHD

Notice that you are now creating thoughts that honor you, thoughts that are grounded in reality and reason. Plus, you are changing your expectations about the future in a way that can empower you.

There is a Taoist idea that this *Ch'i Essential* embraces. It is the significance of what is not there, the absence of something, the Yin.

How did this *Ch'i Essential* change your level of anxiety over the week?

Notice the power that now begins to flow in your life. Anxiety zaps our personal power, creating mental and emotional fatigue. We tend to feel weak and vulnerable when we let our Monkey Mind dictate the future. Do you notice the absence or lessening of the Monkey Mind's effects upon your daily life?

COURAGE

Teach Tai Chi to a Friend or Family Member

IT IS TIME TO SHARE TAI CHI and its positive energy with a friend or family member. Pick a posture or two that you wish to teach the person. Keep it simple. Do not try to teach the entire form.

For those of you using this workbook at home, begin by using the ideas from *Ch'i Essential* 8: Standing, *Ch'i Essential* 11: Non-Shoulder Form, and *Ch'i Essential* 16: Three Ways to Practice Tai Chi All Day Long.

Here's an idea you can integrate in your sharing Tai Chi direct from the Tai Chi Classics called "Walking Like A Cat."

Extremely beneficial, Tai Chi Walking or Cat-like Walking is a very special exercise practiced by people in all forms of Tai Chi. Walking this way focuses your mindful awareness on your root—your connection to the ground, the Earth—which is used to create stability. If you desire to be centered and balanced, both spiritually and psychologically, you must start physically with balancing your body by rooting. In this case that means keeping your weight on the leg that is on the ground.

Most people, when walking, are actually not walking, but doing some form of "controlled falling." Their weight is already concentrated in the

forward foot long before that foot hits the ground. When someone trips and falls, it is usually the built-up, forward momentum that contributes most to bodily injury. Often this result is due to the forward foot having weight in it before it is rooted and connected to the ground. Most falls can be prevented by simply learning to "Walk Like A Cat."

Professor Cheng, in Wolfe Lowenthal's wonderful book *Gateway to the Miraculous*, describes how to Walk Like A Cat as follows:

"Imagine you are walking across a frozen lake. You don't know how solid the ice is. Each step could break through the ice. If you place the foot down with weight in it, you could fall through the ice to your doom. Therefore what you have to do is carefully place each step with absolutely no weight in it. Roll your weight into the foot. Then sit down in that foot and extend the next step with the foot completely empty. Repeat the process with each step until you have crossed the lake."

The *I Ching* also shares a cautionary tale of a fox crossing a frozen pond, adding to Professor Cheng's description that the fox's ears are constantly alert to the cracking of the ice, as he carefully searches out the safest route.

As you play with Walking Like A Cat, keep dropping your weight in the rooted foot for power. Keep your eyes and ears receptive, and allow your head to press against the heavens to engage the Spirit of Alertness that a cat or fox possesses. Keep your movements natural and fluid, adding the element of Flow in all that you do. And remember, do not stiffen up. You already know how to walk. Simply tap the heel of your forward foot on the ground before pouring weight into it.

Remember to share the mindfulness when performing the movements. This is what makes the exercise Tai Chi—the use of *Xin Yi*, the heart-mind to set an intention. Set the intention to relax and nurture your mind, body and Spirit.

Make it fun, like playing a game. Remember the importance of play. We play Tai Chi. Use visualization and imagination to set the *ch'i* in motion. Share the concept of using *ch'i*. Grandmaster Benjamin Lo says, "Use *ch'i*, not muscle."

PHILOSPHICAL CHALLENGES

Much of Tai Chi and its philosophies are counterintuitive to our Western culture. You may bump up against some philosophical challenges that are difficult for many people to embrace.

For example, can you share the celebration of laziness? Most people resist this idea because they were told their entire life that they get an "A" for effort. Help the person with whom you are exploring Tai Chi to discard their Western notions of this concept and instead lift the laziness of the movements to an art form.

Our Western culture teaches us to "try harder" if we want to get ahead. A person known to be a "hard worker" is considered to have a good character trait. Yet Tai Chi should be effortless. Tai Chi trains us to take the easy way out. When we seek the effortless, the movements become more graceful and elegant. The easy way produces less stress.

Seeking the effortless is a challenge mentally for many people. If something is too easy, we do not feel that we have accomplished anything, or that there is anything of value to be gained. Plus, people who do not put forth an effort are called "lazy." No one likes to be called "lazy."

In the beginning, it is hard to believe that each and every movement has the potential to be life changing. How can you share this?

The work that is at the heart of the Tai Chi Form is relaxing and letting go. Relaxation informs everything you do in Tai Chi. When you are relaxed, your body does not fall apart. It hangs together. It is a rational structure.

There is a Taoist philosophy that can help you embrace relaxation. Letting things be what they are, rather than trying to make them something else. When you can accept and embrace this, then you can actually relax and get things done. Trying to make things different from what they are is practicing resistance.

Things work differently in your body as you let go and remove tension and stress. As stress leaves, you move into balance, mentally, physically, and emotionally. Everything works better in life when you are in balance.

Here is a suggestion for explaining the feeling of effortless action. Ask the person you are sharing Tai Chi with to think about a time when he or she was having fun, like hanging out with friends and family. Or to think about a time when the person was entertained, like watching a movie or going to a ball game. When we are enjoying ourselves and having fun, things tend to be effortless. When these things happen, we relax and let go.

Remember, it is not the choreography that makes the exercise Tai Chi. Choreography is just dance steps. Anyone can learn dance steps. Tai Chi is about how you move from one posture to the next. Or, in "Walking Like A Cat," it's all about moving from one foot to the next. It is about how you relax and sink into the ground to initiate pouring weight from one foot to the other, creating both Yin and Yang and stimulating *ch'i* flow. It is about moving with a grace and elegance, like Michael Jackson moonwalking or Gregory Hines performing a tap dance.

REFLECTION JOURNAL TIPS

1. What challenges did you have in sharing Tai Chi and how did you get around these challenges? For example, the not doing and letting go are difficult concepts to grasp for the beginner.

2. What was easier than you thought it would be and why?

3. Did you realize that you actually knew more about Tai Chi than you initially thought you did?

4. Was it empowering to share Tai Chi?

5. What helpful hints can you share that made it easier for you to teach Tai Chi?

6. How did being able to share this art of Tai Chi with a friend or family member make you feel?

Honored Guest

HAVE YOU EVER HAD YOUR feelings hurt? What does that feel like in your body? Like you were sucker punched? Do you become resentful when a person has done you an injustice?

Many of us feel as if we have had our feelings hurt at one time or another. But we know that any time we have hurt feelings, it is merely the ego, or what the Buddhists call the "Self," which is another stealth version of the Monkey Mind.[1] Feeling resentful is a telltale sign that your Monkey Mind is active, and that feeling is feeding your ego, and robbing you of your personal power and *ch'i*. Once you realize this, then true forgiveness can begin.

There is a wonderful Buddhist teaching tale about the very successful Japanese businessman who seeks an audience with a great Zen Master. After patiently waiting several months, the businessman is granted an audience. Upon his arrival, the businessman is ushered into the great hall of the temple. There he spies the Zen Master at the far end of the hall sitting on a pillow in front of two cups of tea. The Zen Master motions for the businessman to join him and have a seat on the pillow across from him.

The businessman sits. After a moment, the Zen Master smiles and asks, "How may I help you, my son?"

This is the moment the businessman has been awaiting for months. Without hesitation he speaks up, "Oh, great Zen Master, please tell me, what is the Self?"

The Zen Master picks up his cup of tea, swirls it around and studies it. After a long moment, he places his cup back down. His gaze slowly floats up, and he locks eyes with the businessman. Wagging a finger in the businessman's direction, the Zen Master crunches up his face, and with a stern voice replies, "That's the stupidest question I've ever heard."

The businessman leaps from his pillow, eyes wide, and exclaims, "How dare you speak to me like that! Nobody ever addresses me like that. I am a very important, successful businessman, owner of a dozen major companies and corporations."

"Forgiveness is the scent the violet gives off after the heel has crushed it."

MARK TWAIN

The Zen Master smiled, and in a gentle tone responds, "Ah, my son, that's the Self. That's the ego. That is the Monkey Mind."[1]

CHANGING GEARS

Let's change gears for a second. Just for the fun of it, ask yourself, if you could meet anyone in the world, living or dead, who would it be? A rock star? Or a movie star? How about the President? Or Mother Theresa? Think of someone whom you would really like to meet.

Next, you hear a knock at your front door. You open the door, and there, to your surprise, is Mother Theresa (or the person you desire to meet). What do you do? Do you leave her standing on the front stoop? Of course not! You invite her inside and your conversation might go something like this:

"Oh, please come in. I can't believe you're here. Thank you for coming. No, don't sit there. Take this seat. It's much more comfortable. Can I get you something to eat or drink? I still can't believe you're here. Thank you again for coming. You've made my day."

In short, you treat Mother Theresa as an "Honored Guest."

CH'I ESSENTIAL ACTIVITY

We know that hurt feelings are a reflection of the ego, the Monkey Mind. Someone cannot take away your personal power unless you participate and allow it. When you come upon someone who is rude or angry, that is a reaction from their Monkey Mind too.

For this "Honored Guest" *Ch'i Essential* activity, you will try an experiment. Tai Chi teaches you to let go of resistance. The next time you come upon someone who is rude or angry towards you, practice non-resistance.

Rather than resist or fight with the person who has treated you with rudeness, you will instead change your energy. Move to a place of compassion. Treat him as an "Honored Guest." See if your positive energy can change or influence the other person or the situation.

Consider the following. Is life more difficult when you lift your energy, or is it harder when you argue and fight back?

Forgiveness is a great way to practice the Tai Chi Principle of Letting Go in your interactions with other people. Forgiveness benefits you not only mentally but physically too. It is a release of tension and stress. The medical community has long known that people who forgive tend to be less angry, depressed, stressed-out, and anxious. Plus, there is the additional benefit of having lower blood pressure and heart rates, especially as compared to those who hold grudges.[2]

"The weak can never forgive. Forgiveness is the attribute of the strong."

MAHATMA GANDHI

Forgiveness does not mean that you have to forget an incident where someone treated you poorly. But rather than holding that negative emotional energy in your heart indefinitely, consider placing a limit on how

REFLECTION TIPS

1.   What did you learn about the energy of forgiveness?

2.   Is forgiveness like Tai Chi in that when we get out of the way and allow it to happen, everything changes? When you allow things to happen, you get to practice Flow and effortless effort.

3.   Have you considered the business applications of treating a client, or your boss, or a co-worker as an "Honored Guest?" You just might make a client for life.

One final suggestion:
Never forgive yourself for not caring or not trying.[3]

long you will allow it to affect you and your relationships. You could very well benefit more from the process of forgiving than the person whom you forgave.

Forgiveness is also a great way to practice the Tai Chi Principle of Letting Go with yourself. Try forgiving yourself for not being the richest, thinnest, tallest, or smartest person in the room. How about forgiving yourself for being afraid? Forgive yourself for not being the most successful, or the cutest, or the one with the fastest time.[3]

"You don't miss your water till your well runs dry."

WILLIAM BELL
MEMPHIS SOUL

Fill The Well

THERE ARE TIMES IN LIFE when you are required to put out non-stop energy in all that you do. This often happens in work at the end of a long project as the due date is quickly approaching. A crunch like this almost always results in a loss of balance. Tai Chi teaches that everything works better in life when you are in balance.

As the semester comes to a close, for most students, energy is moving in only one direction—and that is out. It is crunch time. And this is one of those times when you can very easily get out of balance, causing your grades and your health to suffer. All your work is coming due. Final exams are around the corner. Plus, you need to find a summer job, or internship, or get into grad school. When will it all end?

If you find yourself working non-stop, pushing beyond your limits, and do not take time for a break, you will burn out. If you are constantly putting energy out, your well will run dry. You need to take some time for yourself, to self-nurture, to refill and refuel, and to rebuild your energy.

IMPORTANCE OF PLAY

Let us change gears for a moment and look at the concept of play. People who do Tai Chi are called Tai Chi players. We play Tai Chi. We play ball. Everyone plays music. Elementary schools and most parks have playgrounds. So, why play? What is the importance of play?

Most people play because it is fun. Our hearts and minds, *Xin Yi*, let us know how enjoyable it is to play. You can feel the fun and its energy in

your body. But play does much more than that. Play recharges the Spirit. It brings about the balance of Yin and Yang, work and play. It expresses our inner child and our joy of living.

At the end of the day, play is about discovery. This is how children learn. They learn about movement and their bodies. Children also learn about society and socialization, getting along, cooperating, and being in the world with others.

There is a stealth version of the Monkey Mind that often comes out in school and when learning new things that you need to be aware of. Ask yourself this: In your desire to learn, in your effort to get it right, do you forget about play?

I see this all the time in the beginning of the study of Tai Chi. It is interesting that all the rules of Tai Chi, its movements, and how it is done, were once discoveries that came about through play. The Tai Chi masters would explore. They would explore and discover things like how far the arms go out. How about two more inches? How does that feel? How about two less inches, and what that feels like?

CREATIVE PLAY DATE

It is important to take time to play for fun and discovery. The Fill The Well *Ch'i Essential* is a wonderful way to have fun, restore balance, and build your energy. With this *Ch'i Essential* activity you will have a "creative play date" with yourself. It is the one *Ch'i Essential* where you get to have fun and receive credit too!

For the next two weeks, you will take 45 minutes out of your hectic schedule each week and treat yourself to a date to have fun, and only fun! This is an opportunity to recharge your creative Spirit and your inspiration within.

You will "fill your well" with all your senses—visually and sonically. Use your sense of smell, touch, and taste to reap the full benefits of your play date.

It is important that you do this alone. This play date is exclusively for you, which means no friends. And no pets too! That's right. You cannot take your dog for a run. You can go, but Rocky has to stay home. This is just for you, 100% for only you! You are going to give yourself the gift of 45 minutes of play just for yourself.

CREATIVE PLAY DATE SUGGESTIONS

So what can you do? Anything you like, as long as it is fun and gets your juices flowing. Here are a few suggestions to get you on the right path:

HIT BASEBALLS:

For one of my favorite creative play dates, I went to a batting cage and hit baseballs for an hour. I couldn't believe how much fun it was. I was the only adult there, surrounded by kids and cries of delight. It was an incredible experience. I was elated for the rest of the day.

BOOKS:

If you like to read, find yourself an indie bookstore or a Barnes & Noble. Go in. Browse. Pick up the books. Sit and read. Grab a coffee and enjoy. Explore and discover how much cool stuff is at your fingertips. It is all there for you.

CHOCOLATE:

If you love chocolate, this is a winner. A student shared her experience of going from one candy store to another, chatting with the people at the counter and sampling all the tasty treats. And she did it for free! She told everyone she was doing a project for school, and they were only too quick to oblige and help. Nice!

NATURE:

Nature is a great place to explore, discover, and fill all your senses. Take a walk in a park or the woods. Observe all the colors, smells and textures of the hundreds of varieties of plants and flowers that are there for your enjoyment. Look at things up close. Step back and take a panoramic view. Discover all the magic. Drink it in with all of your senses. Or go to a local botanical garden and explore the more exotic forms that nature takes to express itself and all its beauty.

WEALTH:

As the song says, *"Money, Money, Money."* Ever think about being rich? We are talking "royalty" rich, like a king or queen. You can experience this for very little cost. Go have high tea at the Four Seasons or the Rittenhouse hotel. Bathe in the opulence. Treat yourself to a few of the finger sandwiches. Pick a comfy chair and take everything in. Laze in the lap of luxury for as long as you like and allow yourself to dream. Who knows, you just might be inspired to create wealth of your own.

GO FOR A DRIVE:

Chester County is one of the most beautiful areas, not only in the United States, but in the world. Take advantage of it and go for a drive in the country. Try to get lost meandering on the back roads. Put down your windows. Open your sunroof. And crank up your favorite playlist on the stereo. Drink it all in. I get my best creative inspiration from watching the fields and trees float by outside my car window.

EFFORTLESS EFFORT

The importance of play cannot be stated strongly enough. It restores Flow and recharges the Spirit. With play, you get to practice the Tai Chi Principle of Effortless Effort. Effort is magical and easy when you are having fun.

If you carry only one thing forward into your life from these studies, this is the one I recommend. One creative play date a week for the rest of your life will change your entire journey.

Inspiration[1, 2]

REFLECTION JOURNAL TIPS

After each of your two creative play dates, write a reflection.

1. Notice how your mood and energy has changed.

2. Notice how you feel for the rest of the week.

3. Creative play dates have a wonderful cumulative effect too. What has this *Ch'i Essential* activity done to your balance?

4. Do you feel more in Flow knowing you have that special time just for you?

The primary intention in the beginning of learning Tai Chi as well as in its advanced study is nurturing. The Fill The Well *Ch'i Essential* focuses on self-nurturing. Have you ever considered how important self-nurturing is in your journey through life?

FLOWER

No Judgments

The Non-Judgment *Ch'i Essential*

RAIN

EVER NOTICE HOW PEOPLE REACT when it is raining? How about you? When it is raining, how do you feel about it? If you do not like the weather, you are practicing inner resistance, sending negative emotional energy through your heart and your mind. Once again, we find a stealth version of the Monkey Mind in our self-talk.

Isn't it interesting that rain is considered a sign of good luck in many cultures? In South Africa, rain is considered a blessing. It is a sign of rebirth. It means that the gods are welcoming you and the gates of heaven are open.

In our Western culture, if it rains on your wedding day, that is a sign of good luck for the marriage. It signifies the cleansing of tough times or sadness from your past. In other cultures, rain on your wedding day symbolizes fertility.

So why do so many people think it is a bad thing if it rains? And let's not forget about how people react to winter. It is too cold. Or summer—it's too hot. Which reminds me of the old joke: "It's not the heat. It's the stupidity."

Inner resistance is an expression of judgment and complaining, which is all in your mind. On an emotional level, this inner resistance is negativity, and you can feel it in your body.

"It's not the heat. It's the stupidity."

People often think things should be other than what they actually are, which denies the present moment. It is as if they are denying life itself and the reality of how things are. This is a stealth form of unconsciousness. The next time it is raining, observe how people respond.

I had a neighbor who had tremendous insight about rain and shared it with her two young daughters. When walking my dog in the rain, I heard laughter and shrieks of delight coming from around the bend. As I got closer, I came upon Jesse, my neighbor, and her two young daughters. They were all barefoot, without raincoats or umbrellas. And what they were doing was amazing. Jesse was teaching her girls to jump into puddles of rainwater, making the biggest splash possible. She was teaching them to play in the rain. Can you image if your mother had been like Jesse, and taught you that rain is an opportunity for play? Wow, how would you feel every time it rained after that?

GOOD AND BAD

Let us change gears for a moment. What is good? And what is bad? Stop for a second and think about this. Do you know the difference between good and bad? Most people do, or at least say they do. So why not learn to just do good as opposed to bad? Shouldn't it be that easy?

There is a Buddhist teaching tale about the wise Chinese farmer whose prize stallion ran off and disappeared into the mountains. Later that day there was a knock on his door, and it was the farmer's foolish neighbor. "Oh, you poor man," said the neighbor, trying to console the farmer. "What terrible misfortune rains down upon your house today." To which the farmer simply responded by saying, "Who knows what's good or bad?"

The next day the farmer's horse returned from the mountains with a herd of wild horses trailing behind him as he walked right into the corral. That afternoon the foolish neighbor came running over to congratulate the farmer on his good fortune. "What joy, what wonderful treasures visit your house today!" To which the wise farmer replied, "Who knows what's good or bad?"

The next week the farmer's son went to saddle train one of the wild horses and was thrown, resulting in a broken leg. When the neighbor learned about the son's broken leg, he came again to console the farmer. "What

"Some people feel the rain. Others just get wet."

ROGER MILLER

"There is nothing either good or bad, but thinking makes its so."

WILLIAM SHAKESPEARE
HAMLET

terrible sadness comes to your home," the neighbor exclaims, to which the farmer again responds, "Who knows what's good or bad?"

Weeks went by. Then the army came through the small village, conscripting young men for war. When the army learned of the farmer's son's injured leg, they passed him over. The foolish neighbor immediately went to congratulate the farmer about his son being spared, and again the farmer said, "Who knows what's good or bad?"

When do you expect the story to end?

Good and bad are not absolutes. There is no unchanging "good" or "bad." They are comprised of beliefs, judgments, and ideas based on limited knowledge as well as the inclinations of your mind. Good and bad can then become an activity of the Monkey Mind.

"When you judge another, you don't define them, you define yourself."

WAYNE DYER

NON-JUDGMENT *CH'I ESSENTIAL*

The following *Ch'i Essential* is one of the most difficult to accomplish if you are truly honest with yourself. You are to spend one week without making any judgments. This is the Non-Judgment *Ch'i Essential*. Some of you might have already failed to forgo judgment if you thought to yourself, "This is a stupid activity?" And there you go, that's a judgment!

Judgments often involve measuring things, comparing and contrasting events, circumstances, and even our stuff, creating winners and losers. This involves negative energy being sent through your heart-mind.

Just try having no opinion for a week, a day, or even for the rest of today. This is extremely difficult. Your Monkey Mind is an active animal, changing how you feel about life when you listen to it. Judgment is inner emotional resistance. In Tai Chi you learn to release all resistance.

"People with opinions just go around bothering each other."

BUDDHA

HELPFUL HINTS

Here are some helpful ideas to move you to a place of no judgment:

1. Try this tip to eliminate judging others. See yourself in everyone. Try to find something in each person who crosses your path that reminds you of yourself. Look for their humanity.

2. When someone asks your opinion of what you think about something, simply respond by saying, "I don't know. What do you think?"

3. Remember this, it is hard to know whether something is good or bad. To step into a place of non-judgment, you need to understand the situation's context and time, as well as the limited amount of knowledge you may have about that situation.

"Before you abuse, criticize, and accuse, then walk a mile in my shoes."

ELVIS

"If you can go a week, and not belittle anyone in thought, word, or deed . . . let me know, for I am looking for an apprentice, an heir."

RUMI
SUFI TEACHER

REFLECTION JOURNAL TIPS

When writing your reflection, notice what happens when you are able to stop judging and let go. What does this release of judgment do to the energy in your heart-mind? If you catch yourself judging, simply have another go at "not judging." Push your internal reset button, let go, and try again.

Remember that meditation, consciousness, and mindful awareness are all practices of mental training used to promote a more enjoyable journey in your life. Their positive effects in your life come about through daily practice.

In addition, consider how this experience empowered you when you let go of judgements, if even just for a little while. How did it change your day or interaction with the people with whom you came in contact?

"If you judge people, you have no time to love them."

MOTHER TERESA

During the next week it is okay to have preferences. Preferences are not judgments. For example, if someone asks if you would like chocolate or vanilla ice cream, it is okay to like chocolate. Just do not make liking vanilla ice cream wrong or an inferior choice.

Remember, safety first. Do not walk out in the street without looking both ways. Most people say that is poor judgment. I say looking left and right is playing it safe, and you get to celebrate another day on the planet.

Inspiration[1]

LOYALTY

This Is Water

"THIS IS WATER" IS A WONDERFUL little video that inspired a fellow student to request it as a *Ch'i Essential* for the course because of all the parallels that he noticed. Below is the link to watch the video.

https://www.youtube.com/watch?v=iwEMOt2HTJc

Many of you using this book as a course text are graduating this semester. Congratulations! And congratulations in advance to all you future graduates too! To those of you using this workbook who are not enrolled in this course, congratulations to you as well as a graduate of the school of life.

The "This Is Water" video is an animated excerpt of a university commencement speech by David Foster Wallace, shining insight into the real world and what you can expect down the road.

REFLECTION JOURNAL TIPS

At what moments is the video the same as Tai Chi and the mindfulness we explore to create new possibilties in each of our lives? What specific similarities did you notice? Where else do you notice Tai Chi and its principles in your daily life? What new insights do you have as you go about your daily routine? How has Tai Chi and its accompanying mindfulness changed your journey?

Enjoy the show!

FAITH

Things I Thought I Couldn't Do and DID!

A *CH'I ESSENTIAL* OF EMPOWERMENT

"YOU ARE YOUR OWN HARSHEST CRITIC." Everyone knows this phrase. And it is true for most of us. We are harder on ourselves than other people could ever be, and rightfully so. Self-criticism can be very helpful. An honest self-evaluation of what you are doing or how you respond in a situation is important for promoting growth.

However, the critical voice in your head can, and often is, another version of the Monkey Mind, or what Buddhists refer to as the Ego, or the Self. This is the negative self-criticism, the self-criticism that is not grounded in reality or truth, and no amount of positive or accurate external validation can prevent the harm that this can do to you. This is the self-talk that does not offer any insight for change or improvement.

The way the mind works, especially the Monkey Mind, is that any negative self-talk or self-criticism sets the mind in search of external verification to confirm these incorrect thoughts. And once the Monkey Mind finds this validation, it lets you know that you've really messed up, which again is a kind of negative self-talk. This type of mental activity is not

helpful and often results in an emotional tailspin. The tailspin is another key indicator that your Monkey Mind is hard at work. It creates a downward spiral that sends negative energy through your heart and mind. It is like name calling, which is always focused on hurting, not helping.

So, what can be done about this condition? Is there a remedy for the negative self-talk? The good news is yes. And the answer is within. It is called truth. Your truth. It's your authentic self. The magic of you!

This is the essence of this *Ch'i Essential*, Things I Thought I Couldn't Do—and DID! Ask yourself, what can you do today that you could not do a year ago? Make a list. Think back over the last year. Look at the calendar if need be to jog your memory. What have you tried to do that is new, that you have never done before?

Take a look at all the activities in which you participated over the last twelve months or so. Maybe you made it to the gym three or four times each week for a month straight. Or maybe you burned over 700 or 800 calories on the elliptical, something you never did before. Or maybe you learned Tai Chi, or yoga. Have you tried to sing or play an instrument? Or did you write a poem that moved somebody? How about waking up consistently a half-hour earlier to extend your day? Or, maybe you finished that difficult book you thought you would never finish. Think of all the courses you are studying at the university. I will bet the majority of them, you have never done before. How about graduate from a university? Or comforted a loved one when it did not seem possible?

There are a million things we do that we have never done before, and yet we do not take note of them. I started my own list several years ago, and every time I take a look at it, I'm both surprised and energized.

When the Monkey Mind rears its ugly head, positive affirmations do not last very long. You cannot reason with the Monkey Mind. And metaphysical mantras are not very effective either. Neither is resisting or fighting with your Monkey Mind, deluding yourself into thinking that you are building some kind of mental muscle that will save the day.

Take a play out of the Tai Chi handbook and its principles. Letting go and non-resistance work much better and are sustainable. Let go of your focus on the negative. Turn your attention elsewhere and focus on what empowers you. Look inside for answers, and the answer is your truth.

The remedy for negative self-talk and the Monkey Mind is empowering self-talk, the self-talk that is true! And lots of it! Accurate and positive self-talk.

It is important and empowering to keep track of your accomplishments. When things feel overwhelming or when they feel as if they are not going your way, tell yourself the truth. Your truth. The one that propels you forward.

I suggest you do this at least once a year. Update your list. Add to it. This is your truth. This is the magic of you. Plus, building your list has a cumulative energetic effect that motivates and propels you to reach forward to new places, and toward new accomplishments. Some of these places often are ones you have never considered in the past.

Whenever you feel down or defeated, take out your list and read it. Notice the energy you have created from your personal accomplishments.

Mark your calendar for one year from today and do it again next year. If you would like, send me an email next year and let me know how you made out.   mitch@mitchgoldfarb.com

Inspiration[1]

BEAUTY

Perfect Mate

PART A

HOW WOULD YOU LIKE TO MEET your perfect mate? Or if you have already found your perfect partner, then how about that perfect job, or the perfect volunteer opportunity to serve and give back to your community?

For this *Ch'i Essential*, make a list of all the attributes and qualities you desire in your perfect mate, job, or volunteer opportunity. Be as detailed as you can be.

Is your perfect mate smart? Funny? Does this person have a great sense of humor? Or, is he or she good looking? Sexy? What kind of music does this ideal mate enjoy? Is she or he into sports? Or opera? Is your perfect mate a world traveler? What kind of books does your ideal mate read? What movies does she or he like to watch? What are the mate's values? Does he or she want to raise a family or focus on a career, or both? Take some time and get really clear on what kind of person you desire to enjoy life with.

If you are looking for that perfect job or volunteer opportunity, think of the characteristics of that position. Are you helping people? How do you want to contribute? Is it a nine-to-five situation or a career in which you could set out in the middle of the night on an adventure?

Think about the lifestyle you want to embrace and the work you want to pursue. Maybe you like taking weekends off. Or perhaps you are not a morning person but more of a night owl. Think about geography and cli-

mate, and where you desire to live. All of these factors will give you insight about the jobs or volunteer opportunities you are considering. Perhaps you are a self-starter, a leader, someone who enjoys expressing his or her vision and insights. It is important information to consider all of these aspects.

Make your list as detailed as possible. Be specific. Develop a clear vision of what you most desire in your mate, work, or in being of service to your community or the world. Remember to have fun and dream about the future you desire to create.

MY PERFECT MATE IS:

1. Smart

2. Funny

3. Beautiful Inside and Out

4. Loves to Dance

5. Self-starter

6. Independent

7. Loyal

8. World Traveler

9. Has a Great Sense of Humor & Actually Gets My Jokes

10. Compassionate

11. Family Oriented

12. Loves Dogs

13. Active

14. Athletic

Perfect Mate

PART B

NOW THAT YOU HAVE COMPLETED your list of characteristics and qualities you desire in your perfect mate, job, or volunteer opportunity, take a moment and review it. Feel free to change, add, or update your list.

After reviewing your list, did you notice if you have any of the qualities? Which characteristics do you already possess? Go back now with these characteristics in mind and put a check next to all the attributes, values, likes, and dislikes that you possess yourself. Do not read any further until you have completed this process. Stop reading this *Ch'i Essential* and . . . No cheating! I'll be here when you return.

PAUSE

PAUSE

Okay, I know a few of you probably cheated. That's all right. I won't hold it against you. I couldn't wait to look ahead when I first came across the idea for this *Ch'i Essential*.

Now, take an inventory. How many characteristics do you possess that are also on your list? A lot? A little? It does not matter. Either way, it is important information to consider. Take a moment and think about why you were asked to take a self-inventory. What was the point of doing that?

Many people think the point is to see if you like yourself, which is a good idea, but that is not the main reason. (By the way, I do hope you like yourself. Everyone should. That creates better *ch'i* and energy flow.)

"Thinking makes it so."

WILLIAM SHAKESPEARE

People also think that the point of the self-inventory is to see if "opposites attract." What do you think about that concept? Do opposites attract?

The other side of the coin, the Yin to that Yang, is to consider the "birds of a feather flock together" idea. Are you looking for your bird of a similar feather? Then it's time to read on.

THE SCIENCE

In 2003, the National Academy of Sciences published a research study, which included almost 1000 participants. Each participant was asked to rate ten attributes of a potential partner in the order of importance, and then to also rate himself or herself on the same attributes. The research demonstrated that self-perception matched mate perception in most cases. The results were a "likes-attract" rule for long-term potential partners across a variety of characteristics.[1]

There is an energy rule called the "Law of Attraction" that suggests "like-attracts-like" and that by focusing on thoughts, whether the thoughts are positive or negative, one can bring about results of a similar energetic nature. This does not mean that by using positive thinking you will have the winning lottery ticket. Sorry.

A better definition that helps to clarify this idea is:

"You are what you think, not what you think you are."

Science tells us that everything in the universe is energy vibrating at a variety of frequencies. Each thought has energy. You know and you can feel the difference in your body between the energy of loving and compassionate thoughts versus angry or hateful thoughts. Therefore, consider the Law of Attraction through the lens of energy levels. Energy is attracted to like energy. This is called sympathetic vibration.

We can see this idea of sympathetic vibration affecting similar or like objects in science with the example of a tuning fork. Tuning forks have been used since the early 1700s to tune musical instruments. They are two-pronged, fork-like objects that resonate at a specific pitch to which they are tuned. Striking the tuning fork against a hard surface causes it to vibrate.

If we were to fill a room with a variety of tuning forks, several tuned to each of the various musical pitches, and then strike only one of the tuning forks, say the one tuned to "Concert C," a sympathetic vibration effect would occur across the room. The result is any tuning fork in the room tuned to the musical note "C" will start to vibrate. However, none of the other tuning forks tuned to musical notes different than "C" will be affected.

"All that we are is the result of what we have thought."

BUDDHA

So, what does this have to do with your potential perfect mate? The research from the National Academy of Sciences and the idea of sympathetic vibration both suggest that until you have developed in yourself the characteristics, qualities and attributes you seek in a mate, you will not attract your perfect mate. You will not be a vibrational match to the characteristics of the mate you desire.

Think about this idea. It is not "rocket science." It is easy to understand and easily put into practice. Let us say, for example, that you love to travel, that you are a true citizen of the world. Would that be a match to someone who desires to stay at home and not venture far from their community?

How about if you loved hard rock music? Would that be a match to someone who loves opera? Or if you enjoy the shoot 'em up, go get the bad guy films, and the other person likes documentaries about saving the whales? Or, consider if you like to play sports all the time, and the other person was an avid, stay-in-doors book reader?

The same is true for your perfect job or perfect volunteer opportunity. If you do not like working nights or weekends, some jobs are not a match to the lifestyle you wish to create for yourself.

Consider a few of the following characteristics that could be a match or a deal breaker for your prospective occupation or service contribution: travel, hours, and location. Do you like to work with people or computers? Do you like to help people or solve problems or both? Is it important that your contribution make a difference? Are you focused on earning money? Are you an out-of-the-box thinker, or do you like to have work tasks spelled out?

You get the idea. The helpful information about the "like-attracts-like" rule of the Law of Attraction is that on an energetic level, core values must have a similar vibration. It is not that all the activities in which you engage must match and line up. The true match needs to be based on the underlying values that you and your potential mate possess. Most people's activities reflect these values, and they are a good place to start taking a look when assessing what you really desire in a mate, job, or volunteer opportunity.

Consider cultivating the qualities, attributes, and energy of the person you described as your "perfect mate," and see what happens. Or clarify and be specific about your potential job or volunteer position you seek.

Every single item does not have to be a match, but at least you will understand any trade-offs or compromises going into your choice, which is important information.

Consider the following for your reflection. Which characteristics do you possess already? What did you learn upon reviewing this *Ch'i Essential*? How will this influence your future?

"Thinking without awareness is the main dilemma of human existence."

ECKHART TOLLE

Non-Toothache Mindfulness Practice

"When we have a toothache, we know that not having a toothache is happiness. But later, when we don't have a toothache, we don't treasure our non-toothache. Practicing mindfulness helps one learn to appreciate the wellbeing that is already there."

THICH NHAT HANH

FOR THIS MINDFULNESS *Ch'i Essential*, take three minutes and write down as many of the nonproblems you have in your life at this moment. Do this three times on three separate occasions.

What is a nonproblem? Here are a few examples. When was the last time you appreciated the nonproblem of having a heart that works well and pumps your blood as it should? Or your lungs for bringing the nourishment of the air that you breathe? How about the great job all your organs do to keep you healthy and alive?

How about appreciating the nonproblem of your feet or toes? Did you know that you would fall flat on your face without your toes? Toes are a great nonproblem to have.

What about the nonproblem of the roof over your head? Or how about the relationships that you have with your friends, family, and significant

other, the very people that give meaning to your life? Would this be a good day to call someone and tell him or her that you love and appreciate that person?

Mindfulness and mindful awareness helps you remember to come back to the present moment and appreciate the gifts and blessings that are in your life.

Inspiration[1]

MINDFUL GRATITUDE MEDITATION

Re-read all three of your nonproblem lists at a later date. Bathe in the emotions, feelings and all that you experience. Here are a few reflection tips for you to consider:

1. How does looking at all your nonproblems affect your heart?

2. How will this influence your day-to-day?

3. Are you now ready to go and celebrate another day on this beautiful planet?

Put the answers to these questions and any other insights into your Reflection Journal.

Love Letters to a Stranger

THIS *CH'I ESSENTIAL* IS AN EXPERIMENT in creating and moving energy on campus. And if you are not on campus, then you are invited to share the energy you create anywhere Spirit moves you.

Watch the TED Talk video *Love Letters to a Stranger* by Hannah Brencher. Below is the URL address:

http://www.ted.com/talks/hannah_brencher_love_letters_to_strangers.html

For your mindfulness practice, you will write two love letters just like Hannah Brencher did. Write the letters that you would want to receive, something that would lift your Spirit and motivate you. Write the same kind of letters that your mother or father would write to you. What words would they use? How would they lift or inspire you? Remember, you are moving energy, *ch'i*, on campus and in the world. How much energy can your words create and move in your fellow students? Set an intention, sit down, pull out a piece of paper, and think the entire time you are writing about the person whose Spirit you will lift.

Put your two letters in separate envelopes and hide a copy of each in plain sight. Get creative. Look for that magical place to surprise someone. For students using this workbook, look for a place on campus where they can be found, like in the Student Union, the library, the diner, or the shuttle bus. Address each envelope with the following:

READ ME
This is a
Special Note
Just For You!

When everyone from all the Tai Chi classes participates together, there should be around two-hundred "Love Letters" moving energy all over campus. As a group, consider how much energy is being generated to lift and move people in a positive way.

REFLECTION JOURNAL TIPS

1. Remember to also include copies of your two letters in your Reflection Journal.

2. Write a reflection on how this *Ch'i Essential* made you feel.

3. Reflect on what you thought about when writing your love letters.

4. How did you imagine the influence that your letters and the energy they contained have on the person receiving them?

5. What other ideas about mindfulness occurred to you?

LIGHT

41

Happy Wow Day

EVERYONE LOVES HALLOWEEN. It is a day of celebration for both young and old alike. On Halloween, you not only have the permission but are also encouraged to dress up and wear the most wild and outrageous outfit you can dream up. You get to be anyone you want to be, from a superhero to a ghost. And you get to have fun.

April Fools' Day is a wonderful day where you get to play pranks, practical jokes and hoaxes on any one you choose. Plus, you get away with it. And, of course, you get to have fun.

Both of these special days allows you to do and act in ways that most people repress for the other 363 days of the year.

What if there were one special day of the year where you could do things that made the people around you say, "Wow!" This would be your "Happy Wow Day."

If you could get out of your comfort zone for even just a few hours in a way that benefitted and delighted all people you care about, what would that look like? What would that feel like? And how much fun would it be?

Happy Wow Day is a brand new special holiday where you are encouraged to perform acts of generosity, or bravery, or insight. What if you focused, and practiced, and got up your nerve, and leaned way over the edge of your comfort zone, just for one day? What would you do? How would you delight, inspire, and benefit the people you most care about?

Reflect on your experience of writing your Happy Wow Day description and how you lifted your world and the people you care about.

Inspiration[1]

Lies In Your Head

THE LAW OF ATTRACTION SAYS:

"You are what you think, not what you think you are."

In essence, you become what you think about. Here is another concept about your thoughts.

"You are the sum total of all the lies in your head."

I know that sounds outrageous, but this is how it works. Maybe when you were young, your mom or dad told you, "You can't play the piano." Or Aunt Mary said, "You can't sing. You're tone deaf." Or else you heard things like, "You're not fast enough," or "You're not smart enough."

You get the idea. Other people are often so helpful and eager to tell you what you can or cannot do. As a child you think, "These people are older and smarter than me. And, of course, they love me. They're looking out for me. They have no reason to lie." Then you actually start to believe what they say about your capabilities, or more pointedly, your lack of capabilities. You stop exploring options and you're convinced that what they've said years ago is true. This becomes your self-image. And that quickly becomes your goal filter.

This dualist self-image of what you can and essentially cannot do, sticks in your head and shrinks your comfort zone. The results: It limits you and all the possibilities in your life. But, not to worry . . .

LIFE BEGINS WHERE YOUR COMFORT ZONE ENDS!

CIRCUS TRAINING

Do you know how an elephant is trained in the circus? When the elephant is a baby, trainers tie a five-ton rope to one of its rear legs. The other end of the rope is then staked into the ground. The elephant now has freedom of movement within a circle the length of the rope. The elephant is conditioned to know just how far it can or cannot go. When the elephant grows up, an interesting thing happens. The rope is not changed. A five-ton rope has the confining strength of a thin thread to the mature elephant. It is literally nothing to the elephant. It cannot constrain the elephant's movements. However, the animal has been conditioned to think that it cannot move beyond the length of the rope.

LEAVING YOUR COMFORT ZONE

Have you ever tried to get outside of your comfort zone? What happens when you first venture out? You mess up. That's right. And it's scary. Moving out of your comfort zone is often trying to do something new, something you haven't done before and do not know how to do it yet. On top of that, your Monkey Mind is compounding the challenge by telling you that you can do much better things with your time, things that you are actually good and successful at.

So what do you do knowing that you'll probably mess up when you leave your comfort zone? You apply the Tai Chi Principle of "Letting Go." Do not resist. Accept it. It is part of the journey. This is how we learn new things. This is how we grow. You have a go at it, examine your results, modify your approach, and try again.

When you are in your safe little comfort zone, that is precisely not the time to set your goals. You will be stymied. Why? Because you must believe that there are other options beyond your comfort zone. And you must believe in yourself. You must believe that all the things you are focusing on and dreaming about are possible. You must believe that you can do whatever you put your mind to. After all, that is what goals are, achieving new heights and accomplishments, things you have never accomplished before.

Throughout your entire life you have been told who you are as well as what you can and cannot do. This is your boxed-in, tiny comfort zone. This is your mental conditioning. What you have learned to think "is and is not possible" has become your very own five-ton rope. These are all self-imposed limits. Up until now!

You need to get not only your mind on board, but your subconscious too. If you really believe in yourself, if you really believe it is possible, your mind will work to come up with ways in which you can accomplish anything you desire. Your mind will remove limits and seek out opportunities.

CH'I ESSENTIAL ACTIVITY

For this mindfulness *Ch'i Essential* of self-empowerment, think about all the lies in your head, the ones that you believe are true. Write them down and make a list. Next, convert your list to the positive. Reverse the language of all your lies, and rewrite them as the opposite of what you believe. Use empowering language and present-tense verbs.

Much of the stuff your parents and friends told you about yourself is probably wrong. Take an honest self-assessment. If your mind does not believe it possible, you'll never ever achieve it. Belief in yourself is part of self-cultivation. How Professor Cheng Man-Ching shared the self-cultivation of Tai Chi was to remove fear. And he did that by teaching his students to love themselves.

For the next week, read your new empowering list of what is possible twice each day, morning and night, and read it with feeling. Keep your heart open. You must believe in yourself. Your lies define your comfort zone, and now it is time to remove them and write a new chapter of possibility. The next page offers tips for your reflection.

Inspiration[1, 2, 3]

REFLECTION JOURNAL TIPS

For your reflection, consider the following:

1. How long can you stretch your rope?

2. Are you able to break free of it completely?

3. What did this *Ch'i Essential* do to your comfort zone?

4. How do you feel about trying new things and going after your dreams now?

5. Do you feel motivated?

6. Did you empower yourself to reach for new heights?

Are you going to be a parent someday? Or an aunt or uncle to nieces and nephews? Or a close friend to a family with young children? Maybe you already have one or more of these roles. If so, then what is your message of empowerment to the young people in your life? What positive messages or untruths will you share that will influence these young children into their adult lives? Consider what seeds Pablo Picasso's mother planted in him:

> *"My mother said to me, "If you are a soldier, you will become a General; If you are a monk, you will become Pope." Instead, I was a painter and become Picasso."*

> PABLO PICASSO

"The man who reads nothing at all is better educated than the man who reads nothing but newspapers."

THOMAS JEFFERSON

No Mind Pollution

WHERE DOES YOUR FOCUS GO? How are you spending your time and attention? What goes into your mind without your being consciously aware?

With this *Ch'i Essential* activity of mindful awareness, you will examine what you are putting into your head and the resultant energy that is flowing through your heart. Consider the following:

1. Do the TV, the news, the information in your environment, and what your friends are saying in social media honor you and your Spirit?

2. How does all of this affect you emotionally?

3. Where do your thoughts go given what you are focusing on, either consciously or unconsciously?

MENTAL CALLER ID

For the next week, you will go on a "News Fast," a cleansing of all the day-to-day negative energy that most of us are unaware of.

For one week, you are going to be the "Keeper of the Gate" of your mind. You control the horizontal. You control the vertical. You decide exactly what you let pass through the gate and into your mind. You now have access to a brand new technology I call "Mental Caller ID." Pretend that

your thoughts have Caller ID, and you can choose which ones to pick up and which ones can go directly to the answering machine.

DIGITAL DIET

Now for the kicker. Not only does this include newspapers, TV, radio (what was that?) and Internet news, but it also includes social media! You will be on a "Digital Diet." There is actually a malady called Digital Addiction. Medical reports and research on addiction to social media and technology now use phrases like *Screen-agers* and *E-diction*. So if this *Ch'i Essential* creates some unease, or a physical reaction in your body, then maybe it's time to work the 12 Steps.

"I have not seen a newspaper in three weeks and I am much the better for it."

THOMAS JEFFERSON

IN A LETTER FROM MONTICELLO TO A FRIEND IN PHILADELPHIA

Your Digital Diet includes all forms of social media, most notably Facebook, Twitter, Instagram, LinkedIn, and so forth. If you take a moment to think about it, most of what is posted on Facebook is like the old yada-yada club behind the Junior High School gym, where you yacked about everyone who wasn't present, and not in a flattering way.

A news item on August 1, 2014 had the headline:

> *"The Horror of Facebook Going Down.*
> *You now have to talk to someone."*

I can't make this stuff up!

And that's right all you sports fans, you can watch the game, but you cannot watch sports news. It's news after all.

Why a news fast? Because of the negativity that most people have become numb to. The age-old news motto is:

> *"If it bleeds, it leads."*

A major network offers the marketing line, "Breaking news of the day, sent right to your 'in' box." I wonder if they could send it to my cat's urine box.

FALLING OFF THE DIGITAL DIET WAGON

Not all of you will be able to last a week without flipping on the news or logging in to Facebook. So, if you can't do your News Fast, write down all the negative things you binge on, all the stuff you see and hear, and put into your mind. Look at all the negative energy passing through your head and your heart that you have been unaware of. Notice how you feel when you realize the amount of negative energy you have allowed through the gate and into your consciousness, and include it in your reflection.

If you do not like what you see or hear, what are you prepared to do about it to honor yourself?

Shawn Achor[1], an expert in the field of positive psychology, shared this point about the news on his "Happy Secret" TED Talk, one of our earlier *Ch'i Essential* activities.

> "When I turn on the news, it seems like the majority of the information is not positive, in fact it's negative. Most of it's about

"Every journalist owes tribute to the evil one."

JEAN DE LA FONTAINE
17TH-CENTURY
FRENCH POET

THE WEATHER

Take a look at how the media sells you its weather forecast. Do you ever hear, "Fabulous sunny skies; Great day ahead?" It fact, each of the three major networks have a less than uplifting slogan.

CBS – Eyewitness News: Eye On The Storm

NBC – 1st Alert Weather & 1st Alert Days
(Sounds like the threat level at the airport.)

ABC – Storm Tracker 6

Recently I heard a couple of weather headlines. How do they make you feel?

Snow-vember

Polar Vortex is going to affect 240 million people as far south as Florida.

And last year all three networks introduced a Misery Map. That's exactly how I want to start my day, by looking at a Misery Map. Remember, "It's not the heat, it's the stupidity."

murder, corruption, diseases, natural disasters. And very quickly, my brain starts to think that's the accurate ratio of negative to positive in the world. What that's doing is creating something called the medical school syndrome – which, if you know people who've been to medical school, during the first year of medical training, as you read through a list of all the symptoms and diseases that could happen, suddenly you realize you have all of them."

YOU ARE BEING STUDIED

On October 6, 2014, Twitter and MIT announced that they were teaming up to do a research study. All of your Tweets will be sent to MIT for analysis. The purpose of the study is to discover why social media attracts more negative comments than positive ones.

In an article, *"Munchausen by Proxy by Media,"* Seth Godin[2] wrote:

"MBP is a particularly tragic form of child abuse. Parents or caregivers induce illness in their kids to get more attention.

The thing is, the media does this to us all the time. (Actually, we have been doing it to ourselves, by rewarding the media for making us panic.)

It started a century ago with the Spanish American War. Disasters sell newspapers. And a moment-by-moment crisis gooses cable ratings, and horrible surprises are reliable clickbait (on the Internet). The media rarely seeks out people or incidents that encourage us to be calm, rational or optimistic.

Even when they're not actually causing unfortunate events, they are working to get us to believe that things are on the brink of disaster. People who are confident, happy and secure rarely stay glued to the news.

The media is one of the most powerful changes we've made to our culture/our lives (I'd argue that the industrial revolution and advances in medicine are the other two biggest contenders). And yet because we're all soaking in it, all the time, we don't notice it, don't consider it actively and succumb to what it wants, daily."

I hope you enjoy giving yourself a well-deserved break of "No Mind Pollution" from outside sources for a week. When I watch the news, it quickly becomes my prayer list for the day.

RELIEF IS ON THE WAY

For your enjoyment, listed below are website addresses (URLs) to two positive news websites to help you find your balance of Yin and Yang in the news. The first is a West Chester University Twitter account where you can post compliments. The other is a positive news blog. Enjoy.

1. https://twitter.com/search?f=realtime&q=WCUcompliments

2. http://positivenewsnow.wordpress.com/

HOW DO YOU FEEL NOW?

Here are some typical ways the news focuses your attention. Consider how you feel energetically when you read them.

Consoler-In-Chief was the phrase used to describe our President after mass shootings.

Before the January 2013 State of the Union Address, the address where our President talks about how much progress has been made in our country, the talking heads (our favorite news commentators) talked about what would happen if the President were killed; then what would happen if the Vice President were killed; and they continued down the line, repeatedly focusing on the phrase *"Designated Survivor."*

"It could probably be shown by facts and figures that there is no distinctly native American criminal class except Congress."

MARK TWAIN

"Imagine that you were an idiot, and then imagine you were a member of Congress. Wait a minute. I repeated myself."

MARK TWAIN

EXTRA! EXTRA!
READ ALL ABOUT IT

These are a few headlines designed to fill you with confidence in elected officials, our boys and girls in Washington DC, making our world a little safer:

Looming Political Gridlock: Stranglehold

Government Shutdown

D.C. Dysfunction

Automatic Spending Cuts Take Effect (because Republicans & Democrats Can't Agree on a Budget).

"Government is now something that's not supposed to happen. We're just days away from Sweeping Spending Cuts that could affect your food, your pay. And that's just the beginning." – Meet the Press (FEB 2013)

"Government by Freak-out!" – MSNBC

"From the voters I've talked to, it's definitely a hold your nose election." – Meet the Press moderator Chuck Todd (OCT 2014)

"Opposing the President's policy is not a policy." – NBC *Today Show* stated during an interview with Governor Chris Christie

And finally, if you are not concerned yet with what is going into your heart and mind, I rest my case with this 2014 commentary on the war in Crimea:

"Russia is the only country that can turn the U.S. into radioactive dust."

Now get a good night's sleep, and don't let the bedbugs bite.

"Knowing others is intelligence; knowing yourself is true wisdom. Mastering others is strength; mastering yourself is true power."

LAO-TZU
TAO TE CHING

What Would You Say To Your Younger Self?

ON YOUR ROAD TO BECOMING A "Master in the Art of Living," you know that goal setting does not work well when you are in your safe little comfort zone. You will only get the results that you have obtained before because you will not try anything new. New is outside your comfort zone. It is unpredictable. It is risky.

Getting ahead in life while enjoying your journey includes dealing with roadblocks and obstacles. Roadblocks are a part of the game. Failures and roadblocks are everywhere. But do not give up. Not giving up can increase your joy and your *ch'i* flow. Edison, with his 1000 failures at inventing the light bulb said:

"I ran out of ways to do it wrong."

For this *Ch'i Essential*, you are going to write a letter to your "younger self," sharing all the advice you can muster for creating that special journey through life, one that is filled with joy, love and Flow.

The "you" to whom you are writing could be yourself at age ten. Write your letter to yourself from the perspective of what you know now. Or, feel free to use your imagination and write your letter from the perspective

that you are now age eighty-five. You have the opportunity to reach back in time and advise your current self from the perspective of being a wise elder. What would you say to your "younger self?"

Do we, each and every one of us, have an inner knowing? Tai Chi and Taoism suggest that the answers lie within. We have all heard the phrase, "He or she is an old soul." Treat this as an experiment in tapping into your old-soul wisdom. Don't think – just write. Expect the unexpected. Have fun with what you find. You might surprise yourself. Write your letter to yourself with your intuition, with *Xin Yi*, your heart-mind, giving yourself advice from either perspective.

"What the superior man seeks is in himself."

CONFUCIUS

In addition to writing a letter to yourself, write a reflection on what you experienced when advising yourself. What did you consider? How will having this advice influence you in the future or now?

Remember, in Tai Chi, you are the whole Yin-Yang ball. There is no distinction, just varying degrees of all the sides of ourselves, both hard and soft, playful and serious, strong and vulnerable. You are the entire Yin-Yang ball.

MASTER IN THE ART OF LIVING

"A master in the art of living draws no sharp distinction between his work and his play; his labor and his leisure; his mind and his body; his education and his recreation. He hardly knows which is which. He simply pursues his vision of excellence through whatever he is doing, and leaves others to determine whether he is working or playing. To himself, he always appears to be doing both."

FRANCOISE RENE AUGUSTE CHATEAUBRIAND

"I could change the world.
I would be the sunlight in your universe."

CHANGE THE WORLD
BY ERIC CLAPTON & BABYFACE

Change The World

IF YOU COULD, HOW WOULD you change the world? What would you wish for? What would you invent? Can you use your brain and imagination to turn the world into a better place?

This *Ch'i Essential* activity in mindfulness will enable you to do exactly this: You get to change the world! At first, you will only change the world in your mind. But that's a good thing. Everything is created at least twice. We first create in our mind and in our imagination. Then we put it out into the world.

To start, write about how you would change the world. Do not base your reflective essay on your beliefs of what is and what is not currently possible in the physical world. Take some time and think about the question for a few days before sitting down to write your reflection. Would you invent a flower that could blossom in the snow?

Do yourself a favor and lose your limited comfort zone when writing your reflective ideas. Give yourself a creative gift. Your comfort zone is "I can't." This inhibits *ch'i* flow in your life.

Professor Cheng Man-Ching instructs that the heart-mind, *Xin-Yi*, has the same creative force as the universe, that your *ch'i* is part of the *ch'i* that is the primal energy of the universe.

Wolfe Lowenthal[1] in his wonderful book *Gateway to the Miraculous*, quotes Professor Cheng Man-Ching:

> *"The same ch'i that moves in our bodies is the ch'i that moves*
> *the stars in the heavens. To say that the idea, the intuitive, cre-*

ative power of our heart-mind, directs the ch'i is to say that our heart-mind has in its control the essential creative force of the universe."

Lowenthal continues, stating that . . .

"The professor used to say, a sage sitting alone in his room can change the world. Our minds can control the energy that makes up the fabric of life, all the stuff of our inner and outer reality. This is not magic or "New-Age" fantasy."

ARE YOU A DREAMER?

"Every great dream begins with a dreamer. Always remember, you have within you the strength, the patience, and the passion to reach for the stars to change the world."

HARRIET TUBMAN

Harriet Tubman[2] (born Araminta Harriet Ross; 1820 – March 10, 1913) was an African-American abolitionist, humanitarian, and Union spy during the American Civil War. Born into slavery, Tubman escaped and subsequently made over nineteen missions to rescue more than 300 slaves using the network of antislavery activists and safe houses known as the Underground Railroad. She later helped John Brown recruit men for his raid on Harpers Ferry, and in the post-war era struggled for women's suffrage.

What can you dream of doing to change the world like Ms. Tubman did back at the turn of the century? Notice, she never stopped dreaming and never stopped doing. We all owe her a debt of gratitude for changing the world.

Dreaming is an important quality to cultivate with your heart-mind. Dreams fuel your *ch'i*, and they can and do change the world. The key is not just learning to dream, but in learning to dream as large as possible, as large as you can. Push the envelope of your imagination and embrace the impossibilities.

A fabulous way to start dreaming is to use the opening three words in Dream Number 6 below. *"Imagine a world . . ."* Just finish the sentence. What can you imagine that can change the world?

E.B. White, a wonderful author, changed the world of words. His fascination with words and language, and the correctness of how they were used shaped the way people write and read in this country. Anyone who studies how to write, whether it is nonfiction or novel writing, has or should read Mr. White's fabulous book called *Elements of Style*. He also wrote the everpopular *Charlotte's Web*.

In a *New York Times* interview from 1969, E.B. White said:

> *"If the world were merely seductive, that would be easy. If it were merely challenging, that would be no problem. But I arise in the morning torn between a desire to improve the world and a desire to enjoy the world. This makes it hard to plan the day."*

"Why fit in when you were born to stand out?"

DR. SEUSS

DREAMS THAT CHANGED THE WORLD

Here is a short list of dreams. These are dreams that were large enough to change the world forever. All of these dreams were not based on what was possible at the time; they were dreamed up. See if you can guess who dreamed each idea. The answers are listed at the end of this section. How many can you guess?

1. A computer on every desk in every home.

2. To become the pulse of the planet.

3. To be the best company in the world for all fields of family entertainment.

4. Democratize the automobile.

5. Every book, ever printed, in any language, all available in less than 60 seconds.

6. Imagine a world in which every single person on the planet has free access to the sum of all human knowledge.

But why are there only two choices? How about a third? Why not do both?

The good news is, you can! Simply be your authentic self. Just use your *ch'i*, your personal power to experience the world and savor it. Then put your positive energies out there to change the world too.[3]

TEN IDEAS THAT CHANGED THE WORLD

For your consideration, below is a list of ten ideas that changed the world. I hope they inspire you. Please note that most of these ideas did not exist until some conscious person dreamed them up. Maybe you can dream up the next great idea.

1. Imagine a world without the use of a zero. Someone dreamed up the number zero back in the "fertile crescent" of ancient Mesopotamia, moving us away from fingers and toes as a counting system. Just think, your computer would only be ones without the number zero. Zero is also a wonderful addition to your paycheck if it's on the correct side of the decimal point.

2. The neolithic revolution around 10,000 BCE changed everything. Humans began to cultivate crops and domesticate certain animals. This process of cultivation created the wide-scale transition of many human cultures from a lifestyle of hunting and gathering to one of agriculture and settlement, allowing the ability to support an increasingly larger population. Eventually this made it possible for the Agricultural Revolution.

3. Freud's theory that our unconscious self allows for the study of our behavior and mind.

4. Darwin's "Theory of Evolution."

5. Newton's "Universal Law of Gravity."

THE NEXT IDEA: COMPASSION

How about adding an eleventh idea? What will you dream up that will change the world? How about the idea of compassion? It certainly is one of the oldest concepts around. It's at the core of Buddhism. Compassion

TEN IDEAS THAT CHANGED THE WORLD

6. Einstein's theory of relativity suggested that tiny amounts of mass can be converted into huge amounts of energy.

7. The origin of vaccinations has allowed for the lessening and eradication of diseases thus allowing for longer life spans.

8. The idea of human rights has been on the books for many centuries, but it did not become a universal declaration until 1948 following World War II. As a document it has laid the foundation, not always effectively, of standing up for the rights of all people. Maybe this is a wonderful place to start for your idea to change the world by figuring out a better way for the implementation of standing up for everyone everywhere. We all have to count or no one counts.

9. What about soap? It wasn't until the mid-19th century that a Hungarian doctor, Ignaz Semmelweis, realized that babies where dying at a higher rate when delivered by medical students rather than midwives. Very often the students moved from one task to another without washing their hands.

10. Let's not forget the phenomenon of the World Wide Web as an idea that changed the world.

along with the power of action behind it can help change the world as monumentally as the other ideas listed above. It seems its time has come.[4]

THE PATIENT DREAMER

James Cameron's movie *Avatar* was a dream that sat on the shelf for fifteen years. He wrote out his vision in 1994, but waited because the technology did not exist to make it. Avatar finally premiered in December 2009. How's that for patience and vision, as well as an inspired dreamer?

THE DREAMERS OF THE
DREAMS THAT CHANGED THE WORLD

Below are the answers to who the dreamers were that "changed the world" on the list of dreams above:

1. Bill Gates and Microsoft

2. Twitter

3. Walt Disney

4. Henry Ford

5. Amazon with the invention of the Kindle. But they did not stop dreaming there. Amazon's next dream is almost a reality now. It is the pizza delivery idea taken to the next level. If you live within ten miles of one of their forty-four fulfillment centers, they promise that you can order anything on Amazon and get delivery to your door in thirty minutes or less. How? Drones.

   Note: Amazon's largest fulfillment center is twenty football fields long with six miles of conveyer belts. Pretty impressive!

6. Jimmy Wales, Founder of Wikipedia. Please note that Mr. Wales was offered a boatload of money for his website idea, but true to his word, he decided not to monetize it. In fact, you do not even see popup advertisements on it. How incredibly generous is that!

STAR

Out Of Your Mind!

PROFESSOR GOLDFARB SAYS, *"It is time to get out of your mind!"* That's right, this is your *Ch'i Essential* activity. And no, it is not the same as the college weekend activity in which some students participate.

For this *Ch'i Essential* you are going to get out of your mind at least two times each day for the next week. The goal is to generate presence. We must take ourselves out of our thinking minds to get to the present moment.

Here is a simple technique to help get you out of your thinking mind. Simply ask yourself:

"Am I still breathing?"

Then take a breath. Allow yourself to stop whatever you are doing and just take 10 seconds to be aware of your breathing. By doing this, you refocus your attention away from your thinking mind to your breathing, and then you begin to connect to your body. This takes you into the present moment.

At some point in your Tai Chi practice, you begin to stop thinking about the movements. This often happens with the first movements you learn as they quickly become like old friends. You feel yourself become relaxed, and your *ch'i* begins to flow. Your Tai Chi practice becomes less thinking and more mind. It is thoughtless and mindful at the same time. The mind is what makes it Tai Chi. Application of mindful awareness combined with *ch'i* transforms the exercise from calisthenics to Tai Chi, a moving

meditation. It is pure awareness and effortless attention. This is the desired state. You are just experiencing the moment. Simply being there.

Getting out of your mind is a great way of getting out of your own way. It is like taking a mini mental vacation, which leads to the desired Tai Chi state of relaxed and alert presence. Buddha taught people to understand and acknowledge the true power of their minds. Each and every one of us experiences the world through our mind. As you train and focus your mind on the present, everything changes. Become aware of the power that begins to flow through you. Become aware of the power of your presence.

Inspiration[1, 2]

"Do not dwell in the past, do not dream of the future, concentrate the mind on the present moment."

BUDDHA

REFLECTION JOURNAL TIPS

For your reflection, consider the following:

1.   Notice how you begin to feel after getting out of your mind for several days.

2.   What is changing as you begin to create the habit of generating relaxed and alert presence?

3.   What is different about your day-to-day consciousness?

4.   As you become more connected to your self, are you experiencing Flow in more of your daily activities?

And remember:

    Don't forget to breathe. Breathing is good.

"Everybody wants to go to heaven, but nobody wants to die."

JOE LOUIS

Death Party

CELEBRATE YOUR DEATH NOW—and thus your life! That's right, such a party is a celebration of your life. Throw your own service and after-party. Be there to enjoy it. Plan your own *fun*-eral. What songs would you like to play? Whom would you invite? What food would you serve? Where is it going to be? At a church? Or in a park? How about at the beach?

How will you celebrate your life? For this *Ch'i Essential*, write your own obituary and epitaph. Do it from the perspective of how you would want it to read. Do not do it as your life is up until now. Paint the picture you desire to have. Be open to insights.

Have fun. Life should be a celebration of who you are, what you do, and how you move energy to lift the people that you care about, whether it's your family, your community, or the world. We are all citizens of this planet we call Earth.

Here are a few epitaphs to get you on the right track for your tombstone:

"Pardon me for not getting up."

ERNEST HEMINGWAY'S GRAVESTONE

"Here lies Alfred Stieglitz.
He lived for better or for worse, but he is dead for good."

ANSEL ADAMS
REMEMBERING HIS FRIEND ALFRED STIEGLITZ
WHEN ASKED WHAT WOULD BE THE PHOTOGRAPHER'S IDEAL EPITAPH

"It's never too late to be what you might have been."

GEORGE ELLIOT

You could even write a limerick, like Evelyn Ryan did. She was known as the *Prize Winner From Defiance, Ohio*. There is a book and movie about her life.

> Every time I pass the church
> I stop and make a visit.
> So when I'm carried in feet first
> God won't say, "Who is it?"

"The fear of death follows from the fear of life. A man who lives fully is prepared to die at any time."

MARK TWAIN

Dick Van Dyke[1] was asked by his friend Stan Laurel, the legendary comedian, to give the eulogy at his funeral. Mr. Laurel insisted on writing some of it himself. Here's an example of his thoughts:

> *"If anyone at my funeral has a long face, I'll never speak to you again."*

FEAR OF DEATH

A lot of people are afraid of death and afraid to die. Is it fear of the unknown or our desire to cling to life? In the famous movie, *Little Big Man*, which explores some of the Native American Indian's culture and empowering beliefs, Chief Dan George goes up to the mountain to die. He tells his grandson, *"It's a good day to die."* It is a theme that is repeated throughout the movie.

"We're all dying, some just a little sooner than others."

VINCE FLYNN
AUTHOR

A friend's mom once said that you should not be afraid to die because it will be just like the way life was before you were born.

DEATH AND ENERGY

Let's take a look at death and energy. Your life force is energy or *ch'i*. The first law of thermodynamics is a version of the law of conservation of energy, adapted for thermodynamic systems. The law of conservation of energy states that the total energy of an isolated system is constant; energy can be transformed from one form to another, but cannot be created or destroyed.[2] Does this mean that your energy simply changes form when you pass on?

In addition to writing your obituary and epitaph, include the thoughts and insights you gleaned from this *Ch'i Essential* in your reflection. Starting with the end in mind, how will this influence the goals, choices, and decisions you make in life? Being clear on how we want to be remembered and celebrated can often lead to helpful insights on how you approach the rest of the journey.

Inspiration[4]

"Always go to other people's funerals, otherwise they won't come to yours."

YOGI BERRA

MEMENTO MORI

Walter Isaacson in his book on Steve Jobs[3], included part of the Stanford Commencement speech Jobs delivered. It was about his being diagnosed with cancer and the awareness it brought to him.

"Remembering that I'll be dead soon is the most important tool I've ever encountered to help me make the big choices in life. Because almost everything, all external expectations, all pride, all fear of embarrassment or failure, these things just fall away in the face of death, leaving only what is truly important. Remembering that you are going to die is the best way I know to avoid the trap thinking you have something to lose. You are already naked. There is no reason not to follow your heart."

"Live as if you were to die tomorrow. Learn as if you were to live forever."

MAHATMA GANDHI

Memento Mori was a tradition in ancient Rome. After battle, the victorious General would parade through the streets. Legend has it that a servant would trail him. The servant's job was to repeat to the General, *"Memento Mori,"* which means, *"Remember you will die."* This reminder of mortality would help the hero keep things in perspective and instill some humility.[3]

PEACE

Gap Of Stillness

THE GAP OF STILLNESS IS a wonderful little *Ch'i Essential* in mindfulness that helps to still, and even stop, the Monkey Mind, that incessant stream of thinking.

This *Ch'i Essential* is a lot like the Conscious Breath technique we played with earlier in which you take a conscious breath and feel what happens in your body. You feel your lungs expand. You feel the rise and fall of your chest. With that technique you learned that you could not think and be aware of your breathing at the same time. Conscious breathing stills and stops your mind.

If you were listening to a lecture, and the professor spoke in a gentle, calm, and soothing voice, and then suddenly, without warning, she clapped her hands together loudly and yelled, "Boom," what would your reaction be? More than likely, you would become startled, and maybe afraid. In that very first nanosecond right before your mind could comprehend what happened, before your brain could process what caused the loud noise and why there was a radical change in the tone of the lecture, your thinking mind would stop. Your Monkey Mind would stop. There would be a gap in your thoughts. This is the "Gap of Stillness."

What happens when this gap occurs is all of your attention is diverted and focused on your perception of your environment. You use all of your senses to determine if there is a threat or not. Your habitual stream of thinking stops. Your consciousness is working to analyze what happened. This is how our brains are wired with the flight, fight, or freeze response

to help protect us. Psychology calls this the stress response, which is triggered by perceived mental or physical threats.

The good news is, with this *Ch'i Essential* in mindful awareness, you will not need to be scared to death or face a threat in your environment to stop your Monkey Mind. You can calmly and peacefully trigger your brain in a similar fashion to create a Gap of Stillness in a way that honors you. You can do this visually and wake up the natural investigative curiosity of your mind.

EFFORTLESS EFFORT

The key is to make this *Ch'i Essential* a little game, a short, two-minute game. All you need to do is to look at something without labeling it. That's it. It's that easy and that simple. It's "effortless effort," what you use when playing Tai Chi.

Here's how it works. When you look at something, say a tree for example, your mind immediately searches the database in your head. It finds what you are looking at, and then it tells you, "that's a tree." This happens so fast that you are not aware it's happening at all. Your brain is functioning as a lightning fast computer. Now, once that object is identified and labeled as a tree, and your thinking mind knows what a tree is, your brain moves on to scan for something else. Your consciousness dismisses the tree because it's a known quantity, and then it wanders off, often engaging in your stream of habitual thinking that we call the Monkey Mind.

The interesting thing about your brain is that if it does not find what you are looking at in its database, all of your attention and consciousness remain on the unidentified object. In fact, even more of your senses are dedicated to the unknown thing you are looking at. This creates a similar response as when the professor yelled, "Boom" and clapped her hands together. But the good thing is, this reaction happens without engaging the stress response, which often involves you experiencing fear. Nice! So when you look at something without labeling it, you create a Gap of Stillness that stops the Monkey Mind.

THE GAME

Here is the game part of this *Ch'i Essential*. You will need to use your imagination and creativity to engage your curious nature. For example, if you were to look at a tree, you need to not label the tree in order to fool the database in your head and create a Gap of Stillness. One of the best ways to do this is to find a different point of view, a different angle that is not familiar. So, get up real close on the tree and just focus on its trunk and bark. What does it look like to you from this perspective? Use your imagination and tell yourself that you have never seen anything like this before. Begin to study the textures and intricacy of the bark. Notice the ridges, crevices, and all the colors and shades of greys and browns. Do you see little insects or webs imbedded in the trunk?

As you look at all of this detail, try not labeling what you see. Do not think bark as you look at the bark. Look at it as if you are seeing another planet, deep in the galaxy, for the very first time. Don't label the silk you are seeing as an insect's web. Think of it as an alien's home that you do not understand. Get curious as if you are exploring an unknown territory. Take the time to study and really see it—experience it anew. See if you can create a brief cessation in your stream of thinking. Just experience what you are seeing without thinking about it. Be present and take it all in.

"Between stimulus and response, there is a space. In that space lies our freedom and our power to choose our response. In our response lies our growth and our happiness."

VIKTOR FRANKL

You have now created a Gap of Stillness, a little mini vacation away from the stress of your Monkey Mind. Over the next week, create a Gap of Stillness on three different occasions for two minutes each time. Just look at something without labeling it. Play the game and make the object of your sensory perception unfamiliar to that database in your head. Stop your Monkey Mind by creating a little Gap of Stillness in your thoughts.

Nature is an especially fruitful place to play with this mindful *Ch'i Essential*. The beauty and elegance of what you can experience and observe in nature not only makes this *Ch'i Essential* more fulfilling, but it also makes it easier to do. In addition, with the explosion of technology in our day-to-day lives—smart phones, tablets, and all the devices that connect us to the Internet—there is now a malady called Nature Deficit Disorder. The Gap of Stillness *Ch'i Essential* can reverse its effects and grow your brain, mind, and Spirit with its positive stimulation.

What begins to happen as you continue to create little gaps of stillness is that the gap starts to lengthen and increase in duration. Eventually, as your mindful awareness grows, you become more conscious of these gaps, your inner stillness, and they begin to happen naturally. This is like your *ch'i* flowing when you practice Tai Chi. You do not have to work it.

It's effortless. You just relax and let go and it happens. And just like Tai Chi practice, you begin to open up and create inner space. At this point, the duration continues to increase naturally, and you create a wonderful cycle of letting go and experiencing more and more living in the present moment. Life becomes clearer and more effortless. You feel more alive, and your ability to enjoy the world and your journey increases. You experience, from within, the interconnectedness of all that there is.

With this mindfulness, you are just doing and just experiencing. It's pure awareness, and it enhances everything in which you are engaged, from work and play to your relationships. You enjoy life on a new level, filled with appreciation and gratitude.

Please refer to the "Reflection and Insight Journal" section as a guide for your reflection.

Inspiration[1]

Nine Patterns Of Unconscious Thought

OPENING UP INNER SPACE

THIS IS A *CH'I ESSENTIAL* ACTIVITY for opening up inner space, releasing tension, and allowing your personal power to flow through you.

We know that the ego is a false sense of self, which is often based on mental ideas, concepts, and identification with thoughts. It is exactly these thought patterns that we describe as the Monkey Mind.

What does it mean when you hear the phrase "the ego dies?" This means that you are no longer identified with your thought process as an identity, as a definition of who you are. You know that thoughts are just thoughts, and these thoughts come and go.

Inner space opens up when you let go of your thoughts, the ones you think define you. There are several unconscious patterns of thought that people do not realize are part of the Monkey Mind club. These are the stealth, ninja monkeys, the sneaky little devils that you are often not aware of.

For this *Ch'i Essential*, read over the list below of the Nine Patterns of Unconscious Thought. Once you've detected a pattern within yourself, you will conduct an experiment. Only choose one pattern. If you like this *Ch'i Essential*, you can go back and play with another pattern down the road. It's too difficult to focus on multiple patterns right off the bat. Make it easy on yourself, and pick the one you most identify with.

For the next week, you will discover what it feels like to drop the pattern you chose. Your experiment is to let go of that unconscious pattern of thought and see what happens.

THE STEALTH MONKEY MIND PATTERNS OF UNCONSCIOUS THOUGHTS

PATTERN 1

Did you ever clean up the kitchen, especially the sink full of dishes your roommates (or family for those of you playing at home) let pile up all week? Good for you! Well done. But when your roommates or family got home that night and no one noticed, what did you do? Did you let it slide as they started to pile up a new batch of dirty dishes? Of course not. Then this Monkey Mind pattern of unconscious thought is for you.

DEMANDING RECOGNITION FOR SOMETHING YOU DID
AND GETTING ANGRY OR UPSET IF YOU DON'T GET IT.

PATTERN 2

Often these patterns of unconscious thoughts are easier to see in friends and family members than yourself. Do you know anyone who focuses the conversation on his or her self? It's all about their trials and tribulations, all the injustices and things that keep going wrong in their life. If you see a glimmer of this tendency in yourself, then here's your pattern of unconscious thought.

TRYING TO GET ATTENTION BY TALKING ABOUT
YOUR PROBLEMS—THE STORY OF YOUR ILLNESS
FOR INSTANCE—OR MAKING A SCENE.

PATTERN 3

Hey sports fans. Ever watch the game with a group of your friends? If so, then this pattern of unconscious thought could be right up your alley, and probably some of your friends' alleys too.

GIVING YOUR OPINION WHEN NOBODY ASKED FOR IT
AND WHEN IT MAKES NO DIFFERENCE TO THE SITUATION.

PATTERN 4

Have you ever known anyone who must be seen as the boss, "the answer man or woman," the sole person in charge? Or a person that has to be the coolest one in the room? And of course, that person surrounds themself with people who readily reinforce that image. We all have experienced this at one time or another. This is the next pattern of unconscious thought.

> BEING MORE CONCERNED WITH HOW THE OTHER PERSON SEES YOU THAN YOU ARE WITH THE OTHER PERSON. USING OTHER PEOPLE TO BOOST YOUR EGO OR AS AN EGO ENHANCER.

PATTERN 5

Hey, did you see that Ferrari out in the parking lot? That's my day-to-day ride. You should see my weekend wheels. And check out my flat screen? It's 120 inches, and that's just top to bottom! Boy do I love my stuff, because it's way cooler than anyone else's, and way bigger too. Are you getting the picture? Of course you are. Now you're ready for pattern five of unconscious thought.

> TRYING TO MAKE AN IMPRESSION ON OTHERS THROUGH POSSESSIONS, KNOWLEDGE, GOOD LOOKS, STATUS, PHYSICAL STRENGTH . . . YOU NAME IT.

PATTERN 6

Ever hear anyone rage against the machine? No, no, not the group. I'm talking about someone who gets terribly upset in a gigantic way, bringing attention to himself or herself and the particular situation. This is our next pattern of unconscious thought.

> BRINGING ABOUT TEMPORARY EGO INFLATION THROUGH AN ANGRY REACTION AGAINST SOMETHING OR SOMEONE.

PATTERN 7

Has anyone ever hurt your feelings? Have people ever said anything that has embarrassed or degraded you? If so, you might relate to this pattern of unconscious thought.

> TAKING THINGS PERSONALLY AND FEELING OFFENDED.

PATTERN 8

Has the voice in your head ever complained about how other people don't understand you; that they can't possibly see things from your perspective; that they just don't get it no matter how obvious? They don't get that it's the truth, and you know it. This pattern of unconscious thought is all about that.

> MAKING YOURSELF RIGHT AND OTHERS WRONG
> THROUGH FUTILE MENTAL OR VERBAL COMPLAINING.

PATTERN 9

"Appearance is everything" is a well-worn phrase, but most of us know it is not everything. Yet, almost everyone wants to be seen as or appear to be important. And that is the final pattern of unconscious thought. This one is almost universal. If one of the other patterns are not a match for you, then try this one on for size.

> WANTING TO BE SEEN, OR APPEAR TO BE IMPORTANT.

LET IT GO

Now that you have selected a Pattern of Unconscious Thought that resonates for you, begin to release it. As the song says, *Let It Go.* Just drop the pattern every time it comes up. Notice how you begin to feel. Continue to drop the pattern, letting go of it for the entire week. See what you experience. As you become more successful in releasing and dropping your pattern of unconscious thought, you also become more successful at generating consciousness. The two go together. Begin to discover the enormous power that flows through you out into the world.

For your reflection, consider what it feels like to open up inner space and release the tension that these stealth versions of the Monkey Mind create. De-emphasizing your ego identity not only generates consciousness, but it opens up your inner space.

If you enjoyed the energy and power that you have generated, try another pattern next week. Do this for yourself, for your self-cultivation, and not for this course. But don't announce that you're "free of ego," that your "ego died," because that's ego too. It's just the Monkey Mind chattering again.

Inspiration[1]

Dear Santa

AH CHRISTMAS AND THE HOLIDAY SEASON . . . that magical time of year when you were a kid, and for some of us as adults, too. Remember the anticipation and the countdown of days to that special morning when you opened all your presents. And don't forget the night before, when you couldn't fall asleep, waiting to see if Santa brought you everything on your list.

Those were our formative years when we were kids. No matter what was going on, we had moments in time when miracles abounded and anything was possible, like a fat guy coming down your tiny chimney with an enormous sack of all the coolest stuff your heart could imagine.

Did you ever write Santa a letter? When was the last time you wrote such a letter? In this *Ch'i Essential*, you get to do just that, requesting all the cool stuff you desire in life. Whatever you want. Place no limit on what you dream for or desire in life. However, there is a little twist that requires that you use your imagination to create a truly empowering perspective. Consider this. These are your formative years. That's right. These current moments in time right now are your formative years. Just like when you were a little kid. It doesn't matter what your chronological age is. These are your formative years, and they are forming the future you desire.

Clarify what you want for yourself in the course of the next thirty years. What do you want? Take the next three days and figure out what your "wildest dream" is, and then go beyond that. Complete this sentence, "(Blank) is beyond my wildest dreams."

"All I want for Christmas is my two front teeth."

For example, we all dream about special vacations. Well don't stop there. What is beyond your wildest vacation dream? How about, try living on an island for one year? Do you think that would change your life? If so, then you are on the right path. By the way, living on an island for a year is an excellent opportunity to practice the Tai Chi Principle of Slowing Down.

Once you get clear on what you want and desire in life, then it's time to write your "Dear Santa" letter. Let Santa know what you want for the next thirty years of your life.

I understand that as an adult, you may find it difficult to believe in the same things you did as a kid. In fact, I gave up on the Easter bunny years ago. And let's not forget the Tooth Fairy. She's long gone too. But know this: Santa is real and still very much alive. So have fun and write your letter.

REFLECTION JOURNAL TIPS

After you give yourself the experience of being in touch with Santa, of knowing and feeling that these are your formative years, write down your thoughts in your reflection.

1. How did you feel?

2. Was your head and heart open to the possibility that there is still magic in your world?

3. How much internal energy did you move?

4. And finally, and most important, what gifts, both physically and spiritually, are you open to receiving in the next thirty years?

See The Beauty

"The Buddha can shine out from the eyes of anybody."

JANE HIRSHFIELD
POET

WHAT DOES THIS WONDERFULLY insightful suggestion mean to you? Are we all a Buddha or have a Buddha nature within, bursting to radiate out? Is there beauty in all of us? Can you see that beauty shine?

For this *Ch'i Essential*, you will test this notion and see if you can "See The Beauty" shine in all the people around you. Go into a restaurant or to a park or the library by yourself and look around at all the people. This *Ch'i Essential* works better when you are looking at people you do not know. Can you see beauty in their faces? Or can you see a little Buddha magic shine from their eyes? Be open to seeing the beauty in all that is. Look for it. Set an intention to find it.

Hardly any of us are the perfect airbrushed specimens that Hollywood or the advertising world try to make us believe are real possibilities. We all know what cover-girl beauty is supposed to be. But maybe, contrary to that well-known phrase, beauty is *more* than skin deep.

Have you ever seen a new-born baby or infant? Infants are perfect, beautiful, and nothing but love. No matter what they do, they remain the absolute picture of beauty. They can spit up on themselves. Their hair gets matted down with food. They poop themselves and stink to high heavens. Yet, they are still beautiful and nothing but pure love.

What is the difference between that baby and you? Outside of better deportment and a whole lot better hygiene, there is no difference. We were all born perfect, beautiful, and nothing but pure love. The only trouble is we have forgotten this. Somehow as we get older, we all seem to forget how we started, and the Monkey Mind takes over. When you look in a mirror as an adult, do you see the perfection and beauty or are you focused on all the little flaws, the blemishes, and wrinkles you see? Who is doing the looking, you or the monkeys chattering in your head?

"THE ONLY DIFFERENCE BETWEEN YOU AND GOD IS YOU HAVE FORGOTTEN YOU ARE DIVINE."

Here is a fun little game you can play to help facilitate opening your heart and eyes to see the beauty shine. When doing this *Ch'i Essential*, as you look at all the various people to see their beauty, try to see something of yourself in the person you are looking at. Maybe it's in their smile, or the way they nod their head in pleasant agreement with whom they are with. Maybe it's their relaxed and alert posture, looking connected with all that is around them. Just look for the qualities that you share with them. Can you find something beautiful within yourself that will help you see the beauty in other people?

"Compassion is essentially the recognition that everyone and everything is a reflection of everyone and everything else."

YONGEY MINGYUR RINPOCHE

REFLECTION JOURNAL TIPS

1. Note what you experience in your Reflection Journal.

2. What connections did you feel as you played with this mindful *Ch'i Essential*?

3. Can you see the God force in yourself? Then, maybe you can see it in others too.

"Get your baby pictures out and see the miracle."

DR. BERNIE SIEGEL
MIND-BODY EXPERT

Why not take Dr. Siegel's suggestion to heart? Get out your baby pictures. Hang one up next to your mirror, so when the monkeys come out to blind your vision, you are reminded to look and see the beauty shine within yourself.

Ms. Hirschfield's insight suggests that within any human being, and at any moment in time, we all have access to find what the Buddha found. Are you open to seeing it? Can the Buddha shine out from your eyes too? Consider that what you see is maybe a reflection of your own light.

SPIRIT

*"When you are happy with your life the way it is now,
the whole world belongs to you."*

DR. BERNIE SIEGEL
MIND-BODY EXPERT

You In Six Words

TELL YOUR LIFE STORY IN SIX WORDS
PART TWO

THIS IS A *CH'I ESSENTIAL* INSTANT replay. You get to tell your life story in six words again. But this time let's see how the journey of exploring Tai Chi and its mindfulness has changed your perspective. As an experiment, do not look at what you wrote in the beginning of this workbook. Instead, write your life story, fresh and new.

Remember, there is inspiration everywhere. Even if you do not think that you are a storyteller, you are. You don't even have to write a complete sentence. How does your life look using only six words?

Now, it's time to compare your new "life story" to the one you wrote previously. What new insights did you discover about how you are thinking and processing the world? Have you become closer to connecting to your authentic self? Are you more in Flow after considering the possibilities?

Tai Chi is all about self-cultivation and developing your Spirit. I hope whatever insights and little enlightenments you discovered along the way help to improve your journey through life and make each and every day more rewarding.

Inspiration[1]

HAPPINESS

Some Fun Stuff
A Little Mental Floss to Clean Out the Cobwebs

PART THREE

HEART

53

Growing Your Brain
Lateral Thinking Puzzles

THE LANDSCAPE OF WHAT IS NEEDED to succeed in work and the business environment has radically changed over the past several years. The old model of "Do This, Get That" is not relevant and does not work anymore. The days of going to work, putting in your time, punching the clock, getting that promotion, and then starting the whole process over again to climb the ladder of a successful career are over. Things used to work like that. It was the way of the world. It was easy because you knew the rules. You went to work for the railroad and then retired with the coveted "gold watch" at the finish line. Well, it's time to kiss that idyllic vision of a career goodbye.

"Do This, Get That" was based on linear thinking, predictability, and order. Most education is focused on generating this kind of logical thinking. It is left-brain thinking.[1]

But the world in which we live in today is no longer predicable and orderly. The ever-increasing explosion of technology, computers, the Internet, ease of communication, and access to anyone anywhere, keeps the landscape in flux. It is a tsunami of innovation and change, and it promises to continue increasing exponentially.

How many jobs will the average college student hold in his or her lifetime? The Bureau of Labor Statistics states that the average worker presently holds ten different jobs before age 40, a number that is predicted to grow and grow. This means if you enter the workforce at age 20, that's a new job every two years! Forrester Research, one of the most influential research and advisory firms in the world, predicts that today's youngest workers will hold twelve to fifteen jobs in their lifetime.[2] But what about tomorrow's workers? How many times will you need to reinvent yourself and your career?

What is sorely missing from the success equation is right-brain intuitive and innovative thinking. The good news is that Tai Chi, yoga, and other meditative and mindfulness-based arts help you to grow and cultivate this part of your brain.

HOW THE BRAIN WORKS

This is how the brain works. When you learn a new skill, a little electrical signal gets fired in your brain, connecting specific neurons. The path that the signal takes is called a neural pathway, which is surrounded by a myelin sheath, a protective fatty layer surrounding the nerves. This is similar to an electrical wire's rubber coating. What happens next in the brain is simple. The more you practice a new skill causing your brain to fire an electrical signal on a specific neural pathway, that pathway's myelin sheath grows thicker. The thicker the myelin sheath grows, the stronger the connection in your brain, so it becomes easier and easier to access. Eventually, after enough myelination, you do not need to think anymore when performing this particular skill. You develop ninja-like abilities, often referred to as "mad skills."[3]

HOW TAI CHI WORKS

This is how your brain works when learning Tai Chi. The Tai Chi classics say, "If you want to go left, first you must go right." At first, this advice appears counterintuitive in our Western culture, but think about throwing a ball. The windup, the part where you leverage your body to generate power, is to bring your arm back in the opposite direction of where you want to throw the ball. Hence, move your arm left to throw the ball to the right.

A similar offshoot of this philosophy is the Tai Chi Principle of Slowing Down. "If you want to go fast, first you must go slow ten thousand times." The movement then becomes, what we call in Western culture, a conditioned reflex. This is how you get your mad Tai Chi skills. As you move slowly, with attention and intention, your brain is firing and myelinating a neural pathway over and over again. Then when you need to perform that skill with lightning speed, you can respond to the situation without thinking. Thinking slows down your reaction time. When a person responds more quickly than thinking allows, it is called a mad skill. Tai Chi heavily myelinates the right hemisphere of your brain. This is what is needed for lateral thinking.

LATERAL THINKING

Edward de Bono, physician, psychologist, author, inventor and consultant, coined the term "lateral thinking" in 1967. Wikipedia offers this definition[4]:

> *"Lateral thinking is solving problems through an indirect and creative approach, using reasoning that is not immediately obvious and involving ideas that may not be obtainable by using only traditional step-by-step logic."*

In addition to the study of Tai Chi, I offer the following *Ch'i Essential* activities and puzzles to help you build up skill circuits in your right hemisphere, preparing you to excel in the world we now live in. Plus, in addition to how useful they are, they will improve your creativity. And let's not forget, the most important part is that they're fun!

JOB INTERVIEWS AND BUSINESS MEETINGS

If you sit on a person's left side, you will appear more agreeable. This is one of those left-brain right-brain things[5] that can help with that all-important job interview or business meeting with a client or your boss. Many studies exist that support this idea. Try it and find out for yourself. And in the words of Dale Carnegie, you can *"win friends and influence people."*

It is interesting that when you look at someone, your right brain is doing most of the work. The right hemisphere specializes in faces and is excellent at reading emotions. In addition, the right brain operates mainly through the left side of your body. Your right brain pulls in information from the left of your visual field. This right-brain activity means you will notice more, read more and remember more.[6]

SIGN YOUR NAME IN ALL DIRECTIONS

This fun *Ch'i Essential* activity fires the right hemisphere of your brain. Sign your name. Then write it upside down. Try writing sideways. Do it right to left and then backward. Use mirror writing. Continue in all directions. This *Ch'i Essential* game was inspired by Dr. Jill Bolte Taylor, a Harvard-trained and published neuroanatomist.

THE LITTLE ZEN MASTER

Each hemisphere of your brain has a different personality. Specifically, the right hemisphere specializes in feelings, both mental and physical. It knows things that you are unaware of knowing, because the right hemisphere is more in touch intuitively with your thinking and feelings. This *Ch'i Essential* activity uses both sides of your brain to gain insight and offer solutions from your inner Zen Master.[1]

Take a pencil or pen and write down a question with your right hand. It does not matter if you are left-handed or right-handed; just write the question with your right hand. Ask yourself something like "How am I doing?" Next, switch the pencil or pen to your left hand and write the first thing that pops into your head. Don't think. Write. If you are like me, right-handed, the writing is sloppy and a bit difficult to read. That's okay. It's important that you write the answer with your left hand because your left hand is connected to the right hemisphere of your brain. The answers will surprise you. Your little Zen Master might say, "You're tired. Take a nap."

Have fun with this one. You are accessing your right brain's database. Every time you play with this *Ch'i Essential*, more magic seems to happen.

LEARN NEW MOVEMENTS

Your right brain is needed whenever you move in a new or unfamiliar way. These are the circuits that light up. Whether you are practicing a new yoga posture, or playing with an unfamiliar dance step, or of course you guessed it, learning Tai Chi, you are accessing your right brain and increasing its facility to function and serve you better. Whenever you do any new movement, you are working your right brain. Try walking backward. Try walking with your eyes closed, but please practice safety first. Swing your arms in a different direction than you usually do. Any unfamiliar variation of movement will create the desired effect.[1]

SING

Singing lights up your right hemisphere, myelinates your brain in all the right places (get it?), and is a boatload of fun. Plus, it feels great in your body. It doesn't matter if you're in tune or tone deaf. Just get in your car. Roll up the windows, crank up the stereo, and sing your little heart out. Not only will you have a blast, but you'll come out feeling energized and empowered. Maybe there's even a spot on *The Voice* for you.

EVERYTHING BUT THE KITCHEN SINK

When you have tried everything but the kitchen sink to solve a problem, this one's for you. Let's say you have a problem, a real dilemma where you cannot find an answer. Just follow these simple steps for that right brain flash of insight, your own little Oprah "Ah-ha" moment.[1]

For example, you need to cut expenses, but you do not want to compromise your lifestyle that you love and worked hard to create. Here's what you do. First, focus on your problem. Then forget about it. Read a few paragraphs in several different books or magazines. Next, think of your problem again, and then forget about it. Play with your cat. Get out your binoculars and spy on your neighbors.

Continue thinking about your challenge, and then drop it. Vary your activities in between. Eventually, ideas will start popping into your head. Write them all down and continue with this process. Do not stop and judge your ideas. This will take you out of Flow and disrupt this *Ch'i Essential*. Just keep writing down all your ideas. Not all of them will be gems. In fact, some might be real stinkers and completely off the mark, but if you continue you will access the magic of your right brain and have your "Ah-ha" moment.

When working on a song or any creative project where I need that special insight, I do this activity for several days. I just keep stockpiling all the ideas that pop out, and many of them are perfect for what I'm working on. I've found that the more I use this technique, the easier it is to access the Wikipedia of information and ideas stored in my right hemisphere.

A special shout out to Martha Beck for several of these *Ch'i Essential* activities. Ms. Beck is a sociologist, life coach, *New York Times* best-selling author, and speaker who specializes in tools for empowered living. Here's her example of using this *Ch'i Essential* activity:

> "Dieting made Betsy feel grumpy, bored, and isolated. She and her friend Janet began emailing each other for support, then— ping!—decided to create a blog where dieters could gather to share food fantasies and grumpy harangues. Now Betsy had her ideal body and an Internet community."

Betsy is now helping people around the world to lose weight and feel better about themselves. What magic can you accomplish with this fun *Ch'i Essential*?

Check out Betsy's blog at *www.bitchyourselfthin.com*

THINKING SIDEWAYS
LATERAL THINKING PUZZLES

This is a special category of *Ch'i Essentials* that makes great use of your right brain facilities. Lateral Thinking Puzzles require examination from untraditional and unexpected angles to get that magical ping of insight necessary for their solution. One of the best lateral thinkers of modern times, said:

> *"Creativity is just connecting things. When you ask creative people how they did something, they feel a little guilty because they didn't really do it, they just saw something."*
>
> STEVE JOBS

If you would like a hint at solving and overcoming the challenge of these Lateral Thinking Puzzles, then consider this: The solution isn't what you think it is. Just play with connecting the dots in a new and different way. Have fun playing with these right-brain growers. The solutions are available at the end of this section.

PUZZLE 1
FIVE TOOTHPICKS
Place 5 toothpicks on a flat surface so they form the number 5. Now, without adding, breaking or bending any of the toothpicks, make the number 16.

PUZZLE 2
REVERSE THE PYRAMID
Move only three balls to reverse the pyramid and turn it upside down.

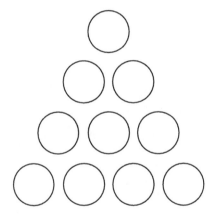

PUZZLE 3
28 DAYS
Which month has 28 days?

PUZZLE 4
WARMEST AND COLDEST DAY OF THE YEAR
What is the warmest and coldest day of the year?

Hint: It happens on the same day every year.

Puzzle 5
FATHER AND SON CAR CRASH

A father and his son are in a car crash. The father dies at the scene. The son is rushed to the hospital. The emergency room doctor is working on the boy to save his life and says, "That's my son." Who is the doctor? (This one was donated by a student. Thanks!)

Puzzle 6
SPEAK FOR ONE MINUTE

Can you speak for a minute without using the letter "A" in any word? In other words, explain the method for talking coherently for one minute, at least 60 seconds, using real words and none of the words can contain the letter "A" in them, upper or lower case.[7]

Puzzle 7
GUESS THE WORD

What eight-letter word starts with "e" and ends with "e," but only has one letter in between?

Puzzle 8
PRIME NUMBERS

Are you smarter than the average geek? This lateral thinking puzzle is part of the Microsoft job interview. Candidates are given three minutes to come up with the proof, the logic and reasoning behind their answer. On average, five out of every hundred could do that.

Prime numbers are numbers that cannot be divided by numbers other than themselves and the number one. Prime numbers are often two consecutive odd numbers, like 11 and 13, or 29 and 31. Are there any examples of three consecutive odd numbers being prime numbers beyond the first ten numbers, and why? [8]

LATERAL THINKING PUZZLES
THE ANSWERS

Thanks for playing. Below are the answers to the Lateral Thinking Puzzles.

PUZZLE 1
FIVE TOOTHPICKS

XVI, the five toothpicks are arranged to form the Roman numeral for the number 16.

PUZZLE 2
REVERSE THE PYRAMID

Check out the numbers before and after the pyramid is reversed. The three balls that were moved were numbers 1, 7, and 10. Number 1 goes down to the bottom center, and numbers 7 and 10 then come up to the top left and right sides.

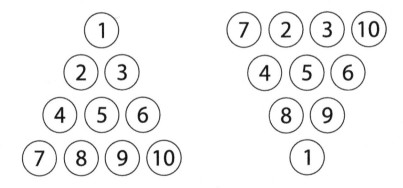

PUZZLE 3
28 DAYS

All of the months have 28 days.

Puzzle 4
WARMEST AND COLDEST DAY OF THE YEAR

January 1st is always the warmest and coldest day of the year. That's of course until January 2nd rolls around.

Puzzle 5
FATHER & SON CAR CRASH

The doctor is the boy's mother. Do you have gender bias?

Puzzle 6
SPEAK FOR ONE MINUTE

Just start counting to 100. You don't hit a letter "A" until you get to "A Hundred and One." But you can even continue longer by counting "One Hundred One."

Puzzle 7
GUESS THE WORD

Envelope

Puzzle 8
PRIME NUMBERS

There are not three consecutive prime numbers. Why? In a sequence of five consecutive numbers, one of the odd numbers has to be divisible by the number 3.

For Your
Consideration
Taking A Look
The Future Is Now

PART FOUR

HARMONY

The Top Ten Skills
For The Future

FORBES[1] RECENTLY PUBLISHED A LIST of the Top Ten Skills needed for the future as reported by the Institute for the Future (IFTF). But the article indicated that these key workforce skills and capabilities are also needed today. With the ever-changing business landscape, what is your ability to adapt?

Interestingly enough, the published information mentioned a Gallup poll that stated: "only a mere 30% of the workforce is actually committed to doing a good job." Here's the good news for both students about to become jobseekers and anyone already in the workforce or contemplating an employment move: if you are "committed to doing a good job," then you are ahead of 70% of the people out there.

Let's take a look at these Top Ten Skills and what we've been playing with using the *Ch'i Essentials* in this book. Maybe you are better prepared than you think.

SKILL NUMBER 1
LATERAL THINKING

Lateral Thinking, or what *Forbes* calls sensemaking. They define this skill as "the ability to connect things to create new ideas." See the earlier section's *Ch'i Essentials* on *"Growing Your Brain"* to better understand how Tai Chi and its mindfulness contributes to this facility in your

brain. Lateral thinking skills are all about connecting the dots in new ways from various disciplines to not only create new ideas, but also to cross-pollinate several of these new and different ideas, creating magic that will contribute to the world. And do not forget the *"Change The World"* or *"Invent One Thing" Ch'i Essentials* too.

SKILL NUMBER 2
SOCIAL INTELLIGENCE

Tai Chi and its Taoist philosophy are about being in harmony with people and the world around us. The emphasis is on the interconnectedness and removing the illusion of separation. This builds Social Intelligence, which is all about relationships and the ability to connect with people. It's about taking a human approach to business, whether you are interacting with an employee, a customer, or a boss. In essence, the *"Honored Guest" Ch'i Essential* created fertile ground to explore and hone the skill of Social Intelligence. It is important to note that Social Intelligence does not mean you need to have all the answers in business. It's about building relationships, which can be done by asking the right questions. But don't forget about the *"No Mind Pollution" Ch'i Essential* and the disconnect from being present and aware of what is happening around you when focusing on social media on your smart phone. Be careful of WMDs—Weapons of Mass Distraction. Being present is Social Intelligence.

SKILL NUMBER 3
NOVEL AND ADAPTIVE THINKING

According to *Forbes*, such thinking means "taking self-initiative to constantly improve your skills, pushing yourself outside of your comfort zone." Does any of this sound familiar? How about the *"Lies In Your Head" Ch'i Essential* and the elephant's rope, not to mention, *"Do Something You Think You Can't" Ch'i Essential*. Need I say more?

SKILL NUMBER 4
CROSS-CULTURAL COMPETENCIES

The *Harvard Business Review* had an article titled, "How to say, *"This is Crap"* in Different Cultures." Marshall McLuhan coined the term "Global Village" back in 1962. Globalization is and has been a reality in business for years. The *Forbes* article states that when "interacting with a multitude of cultures . . . those who know how to empathize and adjust their communications and style of collaboration, will always have an advantage." Mindfulness and meditation builds the muscle of empathy. Just think of the head start you created for yourself with your exploration of Tai Chi, which encompasses both.

SKILL NUMBER 5
COMPUTATIONAL THINKING

Oh no, my brain doesn't work like a computer. Don't worry. That is not Computational Thinking. This skill is "the ability to translate vast amounts of information and data into actual insight." The use of insight simply means that the query "What do you think?" becomes important. This is the essence of your Reflection and Insight Journals: that is, having an experience, gathering information and figuring out what it means to you. It is the ability to understand the meaning of information and to communicate what you think it means.

SKILL NUMBER 6
NEW MEDIA LITERACY

Own a smart phone? How about a laptop or tablet? Then this is one area you do not have to worry about. You are a digital native. Now add the special ingredient of "mindfulness" that you have cultivated throughout this workbook. Not only can you better use these tools to enhance your work skills, but think of all the ways you can improve your work-life balance, Yin-Yang, to promote Flow and harmony in your life.

SKILL NUMBER 7
TRANSDISCIPLINARITY

Transdisciplinarity, which are known as Generalists or polymaths. These are a few big words you can throw around the dinner table to sound smart. This skill is the opposite of using specialists to solve a problem. *Forbes* states that this is the ability to "see the big picture, listen, synthesize ideas and connect the dots," which is very similar to lateral thinking and the *"Lateral Thinking" Ch'i Essentials*.

SKILL NUMBER 8
DESIGN MINDSET

The ability to focus on people when creating products and services is at the heart of the Design Mindset skill. The *Forbes* article states that it refers to "the ideas and attitudes by which a person approaches a situation. It is about focusing on human values and developing a deep understanding of the people that matter most to the problem we're trying to solve." Again, we find another skill that points to "practicing empathy" as the key.

The Design Mindset skill is very similar to the phrase Grandmaster Benjamin Lo coined called "Martial Virtue." Martial Virtue refers to a person's *Gung Fu*, or the skills you acquire through the practice of Tai Chi and its mindfulness. Mr. Lo spoke of attitudes and human values when he said, "Your Tai Chi is only as good as your morality."

SKILL NUMBER 9
COGNITIVE LOAD MANAGEMENT

This is another great phrase to bring up at the dinner table to impress friends and family. All kidding aside, the skill of Cognitive Load Management is at the heart of Tai Chi practice, its mindfulness and the intention you set. Bottom line, it is attention and focus. This is how you do Tai Chi. It is what you cultivate with the use of your mind. With tweets, texts, and emails coming in a mile a minute, "attention becomes paramount." This skill is about managing distractions by effectively filtering and focusing. It's about being present with whatever you are doing or working on.

SKILL NUMBER 10
VIRTUAL COLLABORATION

The global business communities now have the technology and tools necessary to collaborate anywhere in the world. Again we see that the skills of creating relationships and connecting with people, driven by human values, along with practicing empathy are paramount. This is the melting pot of all the skills used in conjunction with real-time video conferencing and much more. It is using attention and focus in a way that causes the tools and technologies to fade into the background when working with the people who matter. In short, do not get lost in your paintbrushes when painting. The focus is on the human being.

Notes and Credits

EACH AND EVERY ONE OF US is an amalgamation of our life experiences, our relationships, and our choices about where we focus our energy and attention. As a result, we all get to stand a little taller thanks to the shoulders of the giants that have gone before us. We can see a little further and shine a little brighter.

The ideas, inspiration, and wisdom in this book are not mine. They are due to the giants who have broadened my view of the world and opened my heart to the possibilities and the impossibilities for this wonderful journey we call life. Whether in person, or through their writings and teachings, we all have access to the giants and the wisdom of the ages that they have so generously shared with us. I thank all you giants and am deeply appreciative.

Included in these Notes are not only a list of the sources of information, but also additional sources that have inspired and stimulated much of the content in this workbook. Credit should be given where credit is due. I have added the untraditional convention "Inspiration" at the end of several of the chapters to acknowledge the contributions that so many people have made, some in person through discussions and their teachings, and others through the ideas and philosophical viewpoints expressed in their work. All of our worlds are larger because of them.

INTRODUCTION

1. Inspired by David-Dorian Ross. David-Dorian is a personal mentor and Tai Chi instructor of mine. He generously shares thoughts about Tai Chi and its philosophies in class, and he is truly an inspiration when it comes to play. Mr. Ross is an International Master Tai Chi Instructor, author, and host of the PBS series *T'ai Chi: Health and Happiness*; he has also collaborated with Jet Li to bring Taiji Zen to the United States in 2014. Trained in China with championship martial arts coaches, David-Dorian has won seven U.S. gold medals, two world bronze medals, and a world silver medal—the highest awards ever given to an American for international Tai Chi performance. Mr. Ross is a Professor with The Great Courses as well as is the Founder and CEO at TaijiFit. (www.daviddorianross.com)

REFLECTION AND INSIGHT JOURNAL

1. Chade-Meng Tan, Daniel Goleman, Jon Kabat-Zinn, *Search Inside Yourself: The Unexpected Path to Achieving Success, Happiness (and World Peace)*, (HarperCollins Publishers, 2014, ISBN-13: 9780062116932)

EVIDENCE JOURNAL

1. Yang Yang, Ph.D., Scott A. Grubisich, *Taijiquan: The Art of Nurturing, The Science of Power* (Zhenwu Publications, 2005, ISBN-13: 9780974099002)

2. Eckhart Tolle, *A New Earth: Awakening to Your Life's Purpose* (Dutton, Penguin Group, 2008, ISBN 0-525-94802-3)

CH'I ESSENTIAL 2: THE TAO: THE WAY

1. Wikipedia, *Tao Te Ching* (http://en.wikipedia.org/wiki/Tao_Te_Ching)

CH'I ESSENTIAL 3: YOU IN SIX WORDS

1. Larry Smith, *Smith Magazine*, writer and editor (www.sixword memoirs.com)

CH'I ESSENTIAL 6: CONSCIOUS BREATH

1. Goldie Hawn, Wendy Holden, *10 Mindful Minutes: Giving Our Children–and Ourselves–the Social and Emotional Skills to Reduce Stress and Anxiety for Healthier, Happy Lives*, (Penguin Publishing Group, 2012, ISBN-13: 9780399537721)

2. Wolfe Lowenthal, *Gateway to the Miraculous* (Frog, Ltd., 1994, ISBN 1-8 83319-13-7)

3. Eckhart Tolle, *A New Earth: Awakening to Your Life's Purpose* (Dutton, Penguin Group, 2008, ISBN 0-525-94802-3)

4. Thanks Mary Lee for the "Red Light Meditation."

CH'I ESSENTIAL 8: STANDING

1. University of Pittsburgh, *About The Brain and Spinal Cord*, Neurological Surgery (www.neurosurgery.pitt.edu/centers-excellence/neurosurgical-oncology/brain-and-brain-tumors/brain-and-spinal-cord)

CH'I ESSENTIAL 10: 29 GIFTS: 29 DAYS OF
CONSCIOUS GIVING AND MOVING ENERGY

1. Cami Walker, from an article "The Giving Cure" in *"Whole Living Body + Soul"* magazine Nov. 2009 (www.29Gifts.org) Cami Walker's book: *"29 Gifts: How a Month of Giving Can Change Your Life"*

2. Lisa's Roses – *Do Something Nice for Someone Today*, Daily Local News – August 2010

CH'I ESSENTIAL 17: DO SOMETHING YOU THINK YOU CAN'T

1. Seth Godin, *The Children's Menu* (http://sethgodin.typepad.com/seths_blog/2014/06/the-childrens-menu.html) 06/30/2014

2. Inspired by CJ McPhee, a Tai Chi classmate of mine. Ms. McPhee is an Energy Moves and TaijiFit Trainer, an inspirational writer, teacher, movement artist, and wellness practitioner. (www.energymoves.net)

3. Goldie Hawn, Wendy Holden, *10 Mindful Minutes: Giving Our Children– and Ourselves–the Social and Emotional Skills to Reduce Stress and Anxiety for Healthier, Happy Lives*, (Penguin Publishing Group, 2012, ISBN-13: 9780399537721)

4. Michael J. Gelb, *How to Think like Leonardo Da Vinci: Seven Steps to Genius Every Day* (Random House Publishing Group, Dell, Reissue edition, 2000, ISBN-13: 9780440508274

5. Alan Alda, *Things I Overheard While Talking to Myself*, (Random House Publishing Group, 2008, ISBN-13: 9780812977523)

CH'I ESSENTIAL 19: THE SWITCH: FIVE THINGS YOU
REALLY, REALLY LIKE ABOUT YOURSELF: PART B

1. Lynn Grabhorn, *Excuse Me, Your Life Is Waiting: The Astonishing Power of Feelings* (Hampton Roads Publishing Company, Inc. 2000, ISBN-13: 9781571743817)

CH'I ESSENTIAL 21: GET CURIOUS

1. Alan Alda, *Things I Overheard While Talking to Myself*, (Random House Publishing Group, 2008, ISBN-13: 9780812977523)

2. Eckhart Tolle, *A New Earth: Awakening to Your Life's Purpose* (Dutton, Penguin Group, 2008, ISBN 0-525-94802-3)

3. Seth Godin, *Why Ask Why?* (http://sethgodin.typepad.com/seths_blog/2012/05/why-ask-why.html) 05/10/2012

4. Wikipedia, *Nature deficit disorder* (https://en.wikipedia.org/wiki/Nature_deficit_disorder)

5. Goldie Hawn, Wendy Holden, *10 Mindful Minutes: Giving Our Children– and Ourselves–the Social and Emotional Skills to Reduce Stress and Anxiety for Healthier, Happy Lives*, (Penguin Publishing Group, 2012, ISBN-13: 9780399537721)

CH'I ESSENTIAL 22: INTENTION

1. Louise Hay, motivational speaker, author, founder of Hay House publishing

CH'I ESSENTIAL 24: MANIFEST MAGIC IN ONE YEAR

1. Bruce H. Lipton, *The Biology of Belief: Unleashing the Power of Consciousness, Matter and Miracles* (Hay House, Inc., 2005, ISBN-13: 9781401923129)

CH'I ESSENTIAL 25: INVENT ONE THING

1. Sir Ken Robinson, *Creativity In School*, TED Talks, Feb 2006 (http://www.ted.com/talks/lang/eng/ken_robinson_says_schools_kill_creativity.html)

CH'I ESSENTIAL 26: FIELD OF AWARENESS

1. Eckhart Tolle, *A New Earth: Awakening to Your Life's Purpose* (Dutton, Penguin Group, 2008, ISBN 0-525-94802-3)

CH'I ESSENTIAL 27: DECLUTTERING: PART A

1. Sarah Ban Breathnach, *Simple Abundance: A Daybook of Comfort and Joy* (Grand Central Publishing, 2009, ISBN-13: 9780446563598)

CH'I ESSENTIAL 30: FIVE QUESTIONS

1. Byron Katie, Stephen Mitchell, *Loving What Is: Four Questions That Can Change Your Life* (Three Rivers Press, 2003, ISBN-13: 9781400045372)

CH'I ESSENTIAL 32: HONORED GUEST

1. Eckhart Tolle, *A New Earth: Awakening to Your Life's Purpose* (Dutton, Penguin Group, 2008, ISBN 0-525-94802-3)

2. Dr. Andrew Weil, *Balanced Living – Ten Simple Steps to a Better Life* (website post 2013)

3. Seth Godin, *Forgiveness* (http://sethgodin.typepad.com/seths_blog/2014/09/forgive-yourself.html) 09/01/2014

CH'I ESSENTIAL 33: FILL THE WELL

1. Julia Cameron, *The Artist's Way – A Spiritual Path to Higher Creativity* (J.P. Tarcher/Putnam 2002, ISBN-13: 9781585421466)

2. David-Dorian Ross: Please see the listing in the Introduction section of these Notes and Credits.

CH'I ESSENTIAL 34: NO JUDGMENTS: THE NON-JUDGMENT CH'I ESSENTIAL

1. Eckhart Tolle, *A New Earth: Awakening to Your Life's Purpose* (Dutton, Penguin Group, 2008, ISBN 0-525-94802-3)

CH'I ESSENTIAL 36: THINGS I THOUGHT I COULDN'T DO— AND DID! A CH'I ESSENTIAL OF EMPOWERMENT

1. Seth Godin, *Self talk*, http://sethgodin.typepad.com/, 03/29/2015

CH'I ESSENTIAL 38: PERFECT MATE: PART B

1. Jean Lawrence, Louise Chang, MD, *Do Opposites Attract?* (WebMD Feature, http://www.webmd.com/sex-relationships/features/do-opposites-attract)

CH'I ESSENTIAL 39: NON-TOOTHACHE: MINDFULNESS PRACTICE

1. Eckhart Tolle, *A New Earth: Awakening to Your Life's Purpose* (Dutton, Penguin Group, 2008, ISBN 0-525-94802-3)

CH'I ESSENTIAL 41: HAPPY WOW DAY

1. Seth Godin, *Happy Wow Day* (http://sethgodin.typepad.com/seths_blog/2014/03/happy-wowday.html) 03/18/2014

CH'I ESSENTIAL 42: LIES IN YOUR HEAD

1. Dave Magrogan, *Rhino Living* Live Presentation 2009 (http://www.cynets.com/dev/flashsamples/rhino/#)

2.   Eckhart Tolle, *A New Earth: Awakening to Your Life's Purpose* (Dutton, Penguin Group, 2008, ISBN 0-525-94802-3)

3.   Wolfe Lowenthal, *Gateway to the Miraculous* (Frog, Ltd., 1994, ISBN 1-883319-13-7)

CH'I ESSENTIAL 43: NO MIND POLLUTION

1.   Shawn Achor, *The Happy Secret to Better Work*, TED Talks (http://www.ted.com/talks/shawn_achor_the_happy_secret_to_better_work.html)

2.   Seth Godin, *Munchausen by Proxy by Media (http://sethgodin.typepad.com/seths_blog/2014/10/munchausen-by-proxy-and-the-media.html)* 10/27/2014

CH'I ESSENTIAL 45: CHANGE THE WORLD

1.   Wolfe Lowenthal, *Gateway to the Miraculous* (Frog, Ltd., 1994, ISBN 1-883319-13-7)

2.   Wikipedia, *Harriet Tubman* (http://en.wikipedia.org/wiki/Harriet_Tubman)

3.   David-Dorian Ross: Please see the notes in the Introduction section of these Notes and Credits.

4.   The list of "10 Ideas That Changed The World" was borrowed from the Charter For Compassion's newsletter (September 23, 2014). Check out their organization, website and the dreams they have for a better world. (http://charterforcompassion.org/)

CH'I ESSENTIAL 46: OUT OF YOUR MIND!

1.   Eckhart Tolle, *A New Earth: Awakening to Your Life's Purpose* (Dutton, Penguin Group, 2008, ISBN 0-525-94802-3)

2.   David-Dorian Ross: Please see the notes in the Introduction section of these Notes and Credits.

CH'I ESSENTIAL 47: DEATH PARTY

1.   Dick Van Dyke, *My Lucky Life In and Out of Show Business* (Crown/Archetype, 2011, ISBN-13: 9780307592231)

2.   Wikipedia, *Conservation of Energy* (http://en.wikipedia.org/wiki/Conservation_of_energy)

3.   Walter Isaacson, *Steve Jobs* (Simon & Schuster, 2011, ISBN-13: 9781451648546)

4.   Stephen R. Covey, *The 7 Habits of Highly Effective People: Powerful Lessons in Personal Change* (Simon & Schuster, 2013, ISBN-13: 9781451639612)

CH'I ESSENTIAL 48: GAP OF STILLNESS

1. Eckhart Tolle, *A New Earth: Awakening to Your Life's Purpose* (Dutton, Penguin Group, 2008, ISBN 0-525-94802-3)

CH'I ESSENTIAL 49:
NINE PATTERNS OF UNCONSCIOUS THOUGHT

1. Eckhart Tolle, *A New Earth: Awakening to Your Life's Purpose* (Dutton, Penguin Group, 2008, ISBN 0-525-94802-3)

CH'I ESSENTIAL 52: YOU IN SIX WORDS:
YOUR LIFE STORY: PART 2

1. Larry Smith, *Smith Magazine*, writer and editor (www.sixwordmemoirs.com)

CH'I ESSENTIAL 53: GROWING YOUR BRAIN:
LATERAL THINKING PUZZLES

1. Martha Beck, *Half a Mind Is a Terrible Thing to Waste* (Article in O Magazine, Nov. 2009)

2. Experience by Symplicity, *Career* Statistics (https://www.experience.com/alumnus/article?channel_id=career_management&source_page=additional_articles&article_id=article_1247505066959)

3. Daniel Coyle, *The Talented Code Greatness Isn't Born. It's Grown. Here's How.* (Bantam Books, 2009, ISBN-13: 9780553806847)

4. Wikipedia, *Lateral Thinking* (http://en.wikipedia.org/wiki/Lateral_thinking)

5. Michael Connelly, *The Gods of Guilt* (Vision Publishing, 2014, ISBN-13: 9 780446556798)

6. National Public Radio, NPR.org, Robert Krulwich on Science, *Draw My Left! No, No, My Other Left! A Hidden Bias In Art History Revealed*, Krulwich Wonders (http://www.npr.org/sections/krulwich/2014/05/07/30982 8787/draw-my-left-no-no-my-other-left-a-hidden-bias-in-art-history-revealed)

7. Lee Child, *A Wanted Man* (Dell, 2013, ISBN-13: 9780440246312)

8. Jo Nesbo, Don Bartlett, *Headhunters* (Vintage Crime/Black Lizard, 2011, ISBN-13: 9780307948687)

CH'I ESSENTIAL 54: THE TOP 10 SKILLS FOR THE FUTURE

1. Forbes Magazine, Business, Reuven Gorsht, *Are You Ready? Here Are The Top 10 Skills For The Future*, May 2014 (http://www.forbes.com/sites/sap/2014/05/12/are-you-ready-here-are-the-top-10-skills-for-the-future/)

"When written in Chinese, the word 'crisis' is composed of two characters. One represents danger and the other represents opportunity."

JOHN F. KENNEDY

HOPE

Made in the USA
Columbia, SC
16 November 2018